THE NARROWNESS OF CONSERVATISM

SHERMA JACQUELINE FELIX

BLACK ADVANTAGE Publishing™

COPYRIGHT

First Edition Published by Sherma Jacqueline Felix

Copyright ©2022 Sherma Jacqueline Felix

BLACK ADVANTAGE Publishing™

All rights reserved. Neither this book, nor any parts within itmay be sold or reproduced in any form without permission.

No part of this book may be reproduced in any form or by any electronic or mechanical means including information storage and retrieval systems, without permission in writing from the author. The only exception is by a reviewer, who may quote short excerpts in a review.

The purpose of this book is to educate and entertain. The opinions and views expressed in this book are that of the author based on her personal experiences and education.
The author does not guarantee that anyone following the techniques, suggestions, ideas or strategies will become successful.

The author shall neither be liable nor responsible for anyloss or damage allegedly arising from any information orsuggestion in this book.

DISCLAIMER

During the writing of this book, Donald J. Trump was President of the United States of America, having been elected in November 2016, officially sworn in, in January 2017, and served for one term until January 2021.

DEDICATION

Dear Church,

I dedicate this book to you.

As you read, you'll discover that the churchisms and personal agendas we've heard at church have little to do with our walk with God, but they have been used as instruments of education and judgement. They are not the answer.

You'll also realize the importance of your inner peace as you process through the elimination of the non-essential religion, political persuasion, and the wrongly divided Word of God.

May the words of this book set your soul free!

Peace & Love,
Sherma Jacqueline Felix

TABLE OF CONTENTS

TESTIMONIALS

"Love is not the answer; love is the assignment." Appraising all thoughts and actions against that profound statement spoken by Dr. Martin Luther King, Jr., one can see where the Church of today; with its proverbial political backdrop, may perhaps be missing their true 'assignment.' Taking Love/Jesus into this dark and weary world is the Church's assignment. Not to be a judge over someone else's sexual preference or a gatekeeper over another woman's womb; nor an instigator of right or left-wing ideologies.

This has caused divisiveness among God's people like never before. Not only is Sherma's topic ripe for such a time as this, but as I'm reading her message through a professional writer's lens, her delivery is fresh and inviting. She superbly uses her inside knowledge, and not hearsay, to break down the reason for the evangelical divide and she shows us how we can heal from it all. Especially during this tumultuous season, this book is a timely tool that engages leaders and congregations alike to have those hard, but much needed, healing conversations."

Terri Liggins, MJ, MBA
International Author, Book Coach,
Ghostwriter and Health Law Advocate

"The Narrowness of Conservatism shares some deep yet simple truths about the political and racial divisions in the Church. Effective communication and uncomfortable conversations are essential in every organization, especially in the Church, and unless these discussions are started, the division will remain. Silence is no longer acceptable. Every leader needs to read this book!"

Danica Trebel
Zig Ziglar Legacy Certified Speaker/
Trainer, Choose to Win Coach

"This must-read book will highlight what identifying labels have done to the Church and how those labels; along with other things have diminished our influence in the world.

As you read, you'll discover the importance of communication between church leaders and their congregations, and how having the hard conversations can narrow the gaps. Any leader desiring strong teams and accelerated results should read this book!"

Pastor Joy Reign
Present Help Ministries

"An excellent read for church leaders and laypeople who are exhausted with the status quo and desire major change. With every chapter, this book provides a way out to fix the elephant in the sanctuary: the great political divide within the Church that keeps us in the mode of status quo. I highly recommend this book!"

Debra Felix
Human Resources Director,
Caribbean Union Conference

"This book is like an alarm clock going off, waking up Christian leaders in the Church about evangelical division. It sheds light on a pragmatic approach to the eerie silence many church leaders can no longer avoid and provides exceptional information for leaders to create strong single-minded saints whom God intended to further the Gospel in unity."

Mary Thompson
M.S., Substance Abuse Counselor

ABOUT THE AUTHOR

Sherma wrote this book so that your soul would be set free from the limiting beliefs of organized religion. She has had her life transformed by the power of God through prayer in an everyday life that continues to give God first place.

With over thirty years of church experience, she has seen what works and what doesn't, what brings confusion and what brings peace, and what causes division and what unites.

A lover of Prayer endowed with a teaching and entrepreneurial spirit, Sherma's desire is to see Christians reject the divisive rhetoric and cling to unity in Jesus. Her books, courses, webinars and teachings have been a source of education, inspiration and encouragement for many.

Learn more about Sherma at:
shermajacqueline.com

FOREWORD

In her book, The Narrowness of Conservatism, Sherma so eloquently reminds us to not get so caught up in what makes us different that we lose sight of what keeps us together:

God. He simply wants our hearts to be after Him. Therefore, it is majorly important to work on our relationship with God; that's the only way to ensure we are hearing His voice versus that of a stranger.

Every day, we have the opportunity to mold our destiny a little more succinctly by virtue of the actions we choose to take.

Unfortunately, too often, people fall into the trap of judging man (what does God's word tell us about that plank in our eye?), while at the same time seeking after man's approval to go this way or that.

We only have to look at the daily 6 o'clock news to see how disruptive and destructive that can be.

So, hopefully, because Sherma's words are opening our eyes to the ways Christians sometimes get off track—be it due to politics, bad relationships, or even getting in our own way with negative self-talk—

I implore you to go into action today to becoming a better and kinder friend, daughter, son, spouse, partner, parent, leader and just all-round great person.

- Les Brown
World-Renowned Motivational Speaker

ACKNOWLEDGEMENTS

I am deeply grateful for the labor of love completed by Maya Angelou, Cecily Tyson and Representative John Lewis as they exuded courage and bravery in realms that I aspire to reach. Thank you for displaying your greatness with levels of humility which are so hard to find!

I applaud the divine dedication of those who have been unwavering in their commitment to tell Black stories: Ava DuVernay, Tyler Perry and Michelle Alexander, whose works have opened my eyes and blessed my soul.

To those who persevered, whose strength I admire, and who continue to exemplify Black excellence without wavering: Bishop T D Jakes, Barack and Michelle Obama, Angela Bassett, Oprah Winfrey, Reverend Bernice King and Reverend Al Sharpton. I am deeply appreciative of all you've done to make the world a better place!

I also acknowledge my children Jevon and Jamilah, my dear sister Debra Felix, as well as the loving memories of Eslyn Felix and Jason Travis Charles, who all have at one season or another kept me grounded, prepared, and ready.

NOTE TO THE READER

This information, including opinions and analyses contained in this book are based on the author's personal experience and research.

There are ten Chapters in this book. At the beginning of every chapter the author highlights different Black women who were murdered because of their skin color and/or sexual preference. This was done to honor the lives and memories of these women.

The author and publisher shall in no event be held liable for any direct, indirect, incidental or consequential damages arising directly or indirectly from the use of any of the information contained in this book.

All content is for information only and is not warranted for any other implied or explicit purpose.

Chapter 1

THE NARROWNESS OF CONSERVATISM

How we got here ...

HIGHLIGHTING BLACK WOMEN:

REKIA BOYD *was a 22-year-old woman who was shot in the back of the head by an off-duty Chicago police officer in 2012. Rekia was walking in a park with friends when an off-duty policeman confronted the group and told them to be quiet. A heated argument took place and as Rekia and her friends turned to walk away, the officer fired several shots.*

During the officer's reckless shooting, a young man was shot in his hand, but Rekia was killed by a gunshot to the back of her head. The officer claimed that he was fearful for his life and that he saw a gun being pulled from someone's waist. No such firearm was ever recovered. The officer was found not guilty of her murder. Rest in peace and power, Rekia!

On March 6, 2017 somewhere between 2 and 3 a.m. as I tossed and turned in bed, I heard the words, "The Narrowness of Conservatism." I mulled it over in my mind for a while before I went back to sleep. About an hour later, the same thing happened; except this time, I got up and wrote it down. When I finally awoke the next morning, there it was again, "The Narrowness of Conservatism." This book is the result of those words. The Narrowness of Conservatism contains my views about the evangelical Church, and the conservative stand embraced by the Church.

It ultimately expresses my views on what reinforcing and keeping that stand has done to the body of Christ, and what it has done and will continue to do to our Christian witness in the world.

It's an in-depth look at what the conservative label has done to the evangelical label, and how these labels as well as others affect the Church, the world, and those who don't know Jesus. I touch on the conservative Church and the different evangelical groups: alt right evangelicals; far left evangelicals, liberal evangelicals, conservative evangelicals, etc. Conservatism has severely narrowed the playing field for all Christians, and we will see how it happened, why it happened, and how to fix it.

I dislike using the words, 'conservative' or 'progressive' when referring to a Christian. I've used the terms in this book only to prove certain points, but in my opinion, we're either following Christ or we're not. We're either Christians or we're not. God's Truth stands out, and His Truth needs no-one to defend it or Him.

The Truth, which is the Word of God, defends Itself. Those of us who believe His Truth don't need qualifiers, because society's qualifiers only continue to divide an already deeply divided Church.

The early Christians walked in the light of the name of Jesus and everything that it stood for. A quick drive through the Book of Acts will reveal that they followed in the footsteps of Jesus as they were led by the Apostles.

Sadly however, as the years went by, identifiers were added to the name of Christianity, then denominations showed up; and now in 2021 it's somewhat of a free-for-all. The body of Christ really had no business being lumped into the category of Conservative, Liberal or any other label, but we did this to ourselves. We are Christians and need no defining labels.

Christian is a state of being, a new life in Christ, a change of heart, a new life of direct fellowship with love and dependence on Jesus Who loved us and enabled us to love Him and others.

The Christian life is not about forcing ourselves into the 'works' of loving others, it is about understanding and receiving His love in us, which then causes us to love others naturally and without much effort.

CONSERVATIVE CULTURE

The spirit of religion has over the years become more and more deeply embedded within the Church without us realizing it. Some of us gradually became comfortable with church rhetoric and the 'thou shalt nots' rather than the actual Word of God, loving God, and loving people. We became familiar with evangelical phrases and euphemisms.

We became at ease with white supremacy, and the oppression of black and brown people groups, even though that was not the way Jesus lived. As a result, there are now racial and political rifts in the church that are so wide that God and only God can fix; and He wants to!

As evangelicals align with political parties, marry them, and have their babies, the main issue then becomes, *"Who and what would Jesus align himself with?"* The culture of conservatism is a very narrow place to live; Conservatism and Liberalism are both narrow places. Confining ourselves to social boxes created by labels is toxic.

We're unable to breathe, let alone think righteously about anything from that narrow standpoint. The conservative label is narrow because it limits who we are; and it places us on the same shelf with other labeled boxes. It restricts the movement of the Holy Spirit and severely limits how and what we hear from

God. The body of Christ was meant to stand out as a light in a darkened world.

As Christians, we weren't meant to be identified by political parties. Unfortunately, now we are. It would be helpful if we all got together to take a stand whenever and wherever conservative oppression reared its ugly head. The problem with that; is that most don't recognize conservative oppression, and if we do recognize it, we don't perceive it as a threat or a problem.

So, we're back to church as usual with the same devils occupying the same spaces they've been occupying for centuries.

From what I've seen over the last twenty-five years, many of us would rather remain doggedly conservative, ignoring the oppression that it causes because it has now become familiar to us.

CONSERVATIVE OPPRESSION

Religion has everything to do with bondage, oppression, or injustice. Any teaching, song, lifestyle, or sermon that attempts to place us back under the yoke of bondage, and under the curse of the law after we've already been redeemed, is considered to be religion. I'm sure you've heard the saying which is all too commonly used. *"That person is so religious."* What that person means by making such a comment; is that the person they're referring to, practices the teachings of the Bible is most likely always at church, and always talks about Jesus every chance he/she gets. That's not a religious person, that's just a passionate Christian. A religious person aims to keep you in condemnation and uses the Bible to do so. A religious person uses traditions, rules, and laws, to replace a genuine relationship with Jesus Christ.

Religion teaches you that you must align with this particular political party or else God won't be pleased, but the truth is that God doesn't want us aligning with anyone or anything other than His Word and His Spirit. Conservative oppression runs its demonic race together with the spirit of religion. The two are inseparable and there is very little difference, except that with conservative oppression the Republican party and its ideals, as well as the wrongly divided Word of God are the tools used to oppress those who oppose them.

Conservative oppression and religion are demonic spirits, whose intent is to hinder and confuse us, while keeping a foot on our necks in order to keep us stuck in a place of deception. When we enter the same space with deception, we can now only see things from our own narrow point of view. Religion is judgmental. It takes pieces of scripture and uses them to make unrealistic rules to live by; this is where the love of God is different. Love says, *"Allow Me to show you a better way, a simpler way."* The love of God doesn't look like the mainstream evangelicalism that is served up in churches today.

DIVIDED EVANGELICALISM

Some Christians refer to themselves as conservative Christians, others are liberal Christians, or Christians of the far right; some prefer the label fundamentalist Christians, or Christian nationalists, the labels are endless. Those different labels are derived from a prideful, need to separate and differentiate one Christian group from another.

All of those different labels say, *"I'm Christian, but I am not like this group over here, or that church over there. I am different (and maybe even better) than them."* No doubt there will be differences between people, because God made us all different for a reason. We are meant to use each other's differences in order to learn from each other and bring balance to the body of Christ but instead, our differences so far have been used to bring division.

Conservative ideology can at times be prideful and uncaring, it's a faith competition and the best faith wins. Those with the best faith get the results, the material things. Those losers with little or no faith are told to tithe, give more offerings, and keep a list of scriptures to confess. Sometimes they're told to fast longer and do other things that have been taught to them in order to show others that they know what faith means, and how it works. It's all a farce though, because that is *not* what faith is and for sure, that is **not** how it works.

Jesus said that they (the world, or those who aren't Christians) would know who Christians were, based on our love (John 13:35 KJV). Our love for each other despite our differences, and our love for the world. At this moment in time, it's difficult to see or feel the love in the thousands of Christian 'camps' in the United States. Especially since we insist on clinging to different Christian labels which further divide and separate us as Christians.

These Christian labels have no real meaning or purpose, they cause unnecessary confusion among the ranks serving nothing but the desires of those in power. The mass exodus of Christians from some churches is not just because of these labels but several other acts of ignorance and demonic oppression have also had an impact. Demonic oppression has so far, successfully served to alienate us from each other for years now, but that is going to change!

DEFINITION OF CONSERVATISM

I once saw a definition of Conservatism on social media that stuck with me. I don't remember exactly who said it, but the phrase was, *"Conservatism is the dread and fear, that somewhere, somehow, someone that you think is your inferior, is being treated as your equal."*

The thought of that being true, makes me shudder. However, the dictionary meaning of Conservatism is: the disposition to preserve or restore what is established and traditional, and **to limit change,** (emphasis mine). During my two-year research for this book, I realized that there were many different faces to Conservatism.

I believe that what we've been dealing with in the evangelical Church is the type of conservatism that at times seems to be about superiority, control, and power. A lot of it is ultra-divisive conservative pride and it often passes in certain circles as the 'God-kind of Faith.' The culture of clinging to labels is one form of conservatism that has persisted for many generations yet seems to now be in the process of being systematically and strategically pulled down by huge invisible hands.

Anyone with eyes to see and ears to hear knows what state the Church is in right now. We could ignore it, deny it, and try to confess it away but with this great divide that we're seeing, the uprooting and dismantling of the religious, pharisaical spirit from within the ranks of the Church, should be the order of the day.

GROUPS, CAMPS, SECTS, ET AL

In some conservative evangelical churches, there are groups known as 'camps'. The camps are different groups within the evangelical circles that think or teach the Word of God differently from each other. If a church doesn't interpret the Bible the way we do, and if they don't do things the same as our church, it's considered to be a church in a different camp. This is another annoying division created for us and by us.

There is a camp for this and a camp for that, everywhere you turn, there's a camp! This is a present day look at the body of Christ and it's important to note that all these groups read the same Bible, but each have different interpretations of what the same scriptures mean. Even among the camps I don't think that we must agree on many things if we can just agree on the one thing, or rather one person, Jesus.

The Church that Jesus has called us to be is not one that is separated by camps or labels: liberal, conservative or otherwise; the longer we persist with these labels, the greater the divide will be. There is a camp called the Word of Faith camp. This is the one I am most familiar with. It's rare to find them preaching in other camps outside of their circles, and they mostly give offerings amongst themselves.

I learned the importance of the Word of God from this group, as well as some really good lessons about

Faith. I've also had to unlearn a lot of things, but such is life. We grow and we learn; right now there is a lot of unlearning taking place as the teaching concerning the Gospel of Grace has taken the place of the religion, we were previously taught.

SHARING JESUS

The question on my mind is this: Does someone have to have a conservative view of politics for the Church to share Jesus with them? Based on the actions of some, the answer is no; but this question arises because we're now in a church culture where the political platform of some churches is wrapped in a Jesus bow!

God forbid that someone wants to accept Jesus but is unable to, unless they also accept the church's conservative belief system. This is just another example of conservative oppression.

It's so subtle how that happens. I don't think anyone is brave enough to say, *"I'll tell you about Jesus, but you also have to accept the conservative views of our church."* It doesn't happen like that. Little by little though, after you've accepted Jesus and have begun to fellowship with believers at a local church, you'll hear pieces of right-leaning politics woven into the sermons.

You'll hear prayers that speak the blessing over one political party and not the other. Depending on which political party is in power, you may (or you may not) hear a prayer for the sitting president.

Pretty soon, based on what I've seen and heard, you're going to have to make the choice to join in with the conservative tribe, or for the rest of your life at that local church, they will keep on showing you from the scriptures just how wrong you really are about your choice of political parties.

Both conservative and liberal leaning churches are guilty of the same thing. It is possible to visit a church and come away with more leftist views than you've ever heard in your life!

THE APOSTLE PAUL SAID ...

I often think of the Apostle Paul, as he wrote in Galatians 5 about divisions and factions within the Church:

Galatians 5:19-21
Amplified Bible, Classic Edition (AMPC)

[19] Now the doings (practices) of the flesh are clear (obvious): they are immorality, impurity, indecency,

[20] Idolatry, sorcery, enmity, strife, jealousy, anger (ill temper), selfishness, divisions (dissensions), party spirit (factions, sects with peculiar opinions, heresies),

[21] Envy, drunkenness, carousing, and the like. I warn you beforehand, just as I did previously, that those who do such things shall not inherit the Kingdom of God.

The Apostle Paul spoke of divisions, dissensions, and factions! Do you think that he knew that in this day, the body of Christ would be divided politically and racially? The Holy Spirit surely did! Those factions were referred to as being practices of the flesh.

Maybe, if we simply looked at things as Godly or ungodly and just or unjust; rather than liberal or conservative, then the discussion could be approached with objectivity.

We can agree with all the truth of the Bible and still miss the power of God. The Apostle Paul knew, by the leading of the Holy Spirit, that we might attempt to reduce Christianity to something we could easily understand. However, the power of God cannot be fully grasped by our brains.

When we attempt to fully explain God to others in order to win them, before we begin, we've already lost. And if we win them to Christ but then attempt to get them to marry into the political party or candidate of our choice, we've lost again.

THE PLATFORM OF JESUS

Jesus doesn't need the platform of the Democratic National Committee or the Republican National Committee. The body of Christ doesn't need those platforms either. If you'd like to register as a Democrat or a Republican because of what their beliefs are, hey… that's your prerogative.

However, God is neither a Democrat nor a Republican. It's because of this dangerous stance that Christianity and evangelicalism have now become synonymous with bigotry, racism, hatred, sexism and intolerance.

The idea that God is either with us or not with us, based on our political affiliation; is one of the biggest lies that evangelical leadership have attempted to shove down the throats of their congregants.There is a level of hypocrisy on the political spectrum that the body of Christ doesn't need to be involved in, yet it seems that we are.

The left (Democrat) does this, and the right (Republican) does that. Why, and more importantly, when … did the Church become involved in being either left or right? We've held on to these labels for ages, and it has contributed and will continue to contribute to the division in the body of Christ.

There's also the propensity to cast stones at those we perceive to be sinners, rather than expressing the love of Christ. As we search for sins to condemn and people to persecute, all in the name of God, we must realize that this is simply the enemy's modus operandi that keeps us from seeing that which is kind, lovely, and of good report.

If the enemy can continue to cause division in the Church by using those whom he has already groomed to hate, then he can continue to incite hatred in the Church. In Word of Faith circles the division used to be simpler. You either had 'stuff,' or you didn't. Those who were good Christians did their confessions, volunteered at church, gave the tithe, and learnt the scriptures; and they were the only ones who were supposed to receive from God; except, it wasn't so at all.

However, even though that line is still visible in those circles, there's also another division between the liberals and the conservatives. Those who consider themselves liberals view the conservatives as uncaring, while the conservatives view the liberals as people who don't uphold Biblical principles, and who may or may not get to heaven based on their views concerning Israel, abortion, immigration, and Black Lives Matter.

The more I watched and listened, the less interested I became in the politics of the Church and the political stance of the Church, both from the pulpit as well as behind the scenes. It seemed to me back then, that even if you disagree just a little bit with other conservatives you may as well be liberal, because there is a sectarian culture that doesn't allow for disagreement in some conservative circles.

As a child, I grew up in a church that was embalmed with religion. We focused on what we couldn't eat, what we couldn't drink, what we couldn't wear; and where we couldn't go.

I wanted my ears pierced, I wanted to attend parties, and wear jewelry. I wanted out of that church! Eventually I did get out, promising myself never to ever return to religion; except, I didn't know that it was religion at the time. I just knew that the rules, restrictions and oppression didn't sit well with me. I figured that the further I could get away from that, the better I would feel and the freer I would be. I was right. We must love the least of these and call out hypocrisy and self-righteousness that have poisoned our pews because any people are done with the Jesus that they are **not** seeing in the words and actions of fellow Christians.

Our churches are filled with 'church people,' people who know how to do church, are familiar with the Word of God, and speak the Christian language. Unfortunately, you won't know some in this group by their unconditional love for all mankind. You'll probably recognize them as those who have lowered standards and morals in order to grab election wins.

Somehow, this group has now become the loudest voice for the Church! As a result, there are many in the world that won't even listen to what we have to say anymore. New Christians are staying away from church, and multiplied thousands began worshipping at home by themselves even before the Corona virus began. The Church is in crisis mode. Thank God, it is fixable!

CONSERVATISM'S NARROW LANE

For the Body of Christ, conservatism is a narrow place to live because of the restrictions it places on us (as stated earlier). It also has exposed every bit of control, oppression, racism, sexism, bigotry and religious extremism that it could find. I'm not sure that the Church at large has recognized this because in most sanctuaries we're still conducting business as usual, with church leadership planning their biennial sermons on 'How to Vote and Why'.

When the leadership at evangelical churches use their platforms to justify the political party of their choice in order to secure a win at the next election, it's not just the congregation that's watching but also the world. So is God. As a result there are large groups of people who only wanted to hear about Jesus and the Word of God, that were just alienated based on religious rhetoric. It's disgraceful and rude to attempt to upstage God by shifting focus to your favorite political party!

Since all Conservatism isn't right-wing, and all Liberalism isn't left-wing, it has now become more important than ever to cling to the words of Jesus when He admonished us to love each other. Your political opponent is not your enemy in the eyes of God. There's one enemy, the only enemy is Satan.

Maybe he is using someone to get to you, but the person is not the enemy, Satan is. The finger-pointing done by both left and right-wing advocates in the church does nothing to change the view of the Church in the eyes of the world. In fact, it squeezes us into an even narrower space.

THE CHURCH AS AN OPPRESSED MINORITY

I've heard the narrative of the Church being the oppressed minority, and that narrative is just about as real as the unicorn hiding beneath your bed.

The marginalized conservative is yet another narrow place of evangelical conservatism; no one is persecuting the Church in the United States of America.

If you'd like to witness persecution, go to foreign nations where your head could be chopped off for believing in Jesus. If Starbucks doesn't have your favorite Christmas cups, or you feel marginalized because the Ten Commandments aren't being placed back in schools; that does not count as persecution!

Who wants the Ten Commandments placed anywhere anyway? Didn't Jesus give us one commandment that would take care of all the others? He told us to love one another. Did He come to fulfill the law? Yes, He did. The Church is not an oppressed minority.

Rather it seems to be quite the opposite, that some in the church are the ones who oppress minorities! If we continue to preach the Gospel within the narrow limits of conservatism, we will be extremely useful to those with political agendas, but we will be of no use in the Kingdom of God and of His Christ.

Chapter 2

THE EVANGELICAL CHURCH

HIGHLIGHTING BLACK WOMEN:

ATATIANA JEFFERSON *was a 28-year-old woman who was shot by police in Ft Worth Texas when an officer was responding to a request for a welfare check. The officer previously exhibited a pattern of escalating encounters with the public. He was indicted by a grand jury on a murder charge in December 2019. Rest in peace and power, Atatiana!*

The late great Reverend Billy Graham, in an interview in a February 1, 1981 cover story in Parade Magazine, said, *"I don't want to see religious bigotry in any form. Liberals organized in the '60s, and conservatives certainly have a right to organize in the '80s, but it would disturb me if there was a wedding between the religious fundamentalists and the political right. The hard right has no interest in religion except to manipulate it."*

The word Evangelical used to be the word that was associated with women and men who took a stand on the Word of God and walked the high moral ground.

But a lot of what now passes for American Christianity is very far from being Biblical. It starts with taking the scriptures completely out of context, and it goes all the way to sometimes placing the financial prosperity of the believer above their relationship with Jesus.

Evangelicals who were once considered the moral majority were found to be swinging with whomever headed up their favorite political party. We either attended a church that supported a specific political party, or we attended one that didn't mind telling us what they didn't like about either party. In the interim, some congregations were duped.

We showed up at church to hear about Jesus, and we never even heard His name, but we did learn about who the Pastor's favorite candidate was, and who would be the next president of the United States based on the Pastor's prophetic utterances.

When someone takes the Word of God out of context to justify their righteous position, you know you're talking to someone who has an unrighteous agenda. Christianity loves and accepts all people and doesn't need an agenda to sway people one way or the other.

Just preach Jesus, Him we preach!

If we're not people who are trying to live like Jesus Christ, with a humble and teachable spirit, busying ourselves with serving and loving others, then we're probably narrow-minded evangelical conservatives, living out of a box of narrow beliefs that shut out those who don't look, dress, act, vote, and live like us; or maybe we're somewhere in between. There are a lot of things floating around conservative evangelical circles that we must unlearn:

- You and I are not exempt from trials because we know how to pray prayers from the Word of God.
- God bless America is not in the Bible.
- Jesus isn't good only to Republicans.
- Regardless of our self-perceived righteousness, our denomination isn't the only one making it into heaven.
- Non denomination is a denomination. Word of Faith *is* a denomination.
- Our faith cannot be contaminated. Why?
  Because it was born out of incorruptible seed, and **an incorruptible seed will always produce an incorruptible fruit**.
  Since Faith is a supernatural fruit of the Spirit that was born out of the seed that is incorruptible, your Faith is also incorruptible, and therefore not ever able to be contaminated.

- If we neglect to give the tithe we're not going to be placed back under the curse. Let me repeat, if you do not give the tithe, you are *not* going to be placed back under the curse of the law. Jesus has already taken care of the curse for you!

EVANGELICAL RELIGION

Wrongly dividing the Word of Truth, cherry picking at the scriptures, and elevating our *'camp'* above everyone else's, does more harm than good to the body of Christ. Because we pray in a manner that is different to other churches, it doesn't mean that our way elevates us above them.

It just means that we pray in a different manner, that's all! The fact that someone used 100 scriptures and prayed them every day for a year, and they were healed, doesn't mean that everyone should do the same thing. Somehow, we've taken individual experiences and testimonies and turned them into doctrine for the Church.

If we're driven by our works:

- how many times we pray;
- how many scriptures we confess;
- how many times we attend church per week;

Then that's a clue that we may be well on our way to becoming a narrow-minded conservative evangelical.

If your church tells you that you should do certain things such as the works I listed above, in order to qualify for the Blessing of God, or for the curse to leave your house, etc. I need you to know that you're being lied to.

The borders of trust have been broken in the Church. A lot of congregants don't trust their Pastors anymore, and many feel betrayed. Pre Covid-19, many attended church out of duty and responsibility. Maybe it would have been better for us to stay at home, rather than sit at church with poisonous thoughts and judgmental spirits, while reliving the scenarios that broke our trust in the first place.

We do believe that we have freedom of religion in the United States but the way it's played out is: 'You have Freedom of religion, as long as it's my religion'. Denominations may be where the great divide began but everyone doesn't have to agree on everything for us to make it into heaven.

If our denominations all looked to Jesus, rather than pointing out each other's differences, I'm pretty sure that we could get the job done and mend the rift! Some churches believe that you only get to heaven if you hold worship services on a particular day of the week, while other churches believe that it doesn't matter what day you worship. Some churches believe that we should pray to Mary as the mother of Jesus and participate in worshipping and honoring the saints of the Bible, while other churches don't. Some churches teach that God will put sickness on your body to teach you a lesson.

Other churches believe that God would never do that, but He will cause you to be broke because you didn't give the tithe. With all these different teachings originating out of the same Bible, it isn't a surprise that there is so much division within the Church. Many people don't even know what to believe anymore! Could it be that all we want when we show up at a church service is for our leaders to teach us the Word, teach us how to be led by the Holy Spirit and keep their personal political passions out of it?

For sure there is a place for Christians in politics, and it would be ideal if more Christians were involved in the political process, but if my Pastor teaches me how to hear and follow the Holy Spirit, I'll know how to vote!

I won't need him to pummel me twice a week by preaching about how much the life of his favorite candidate lines up with the Word of God. Teach me how to hear God and then let me hear Him for myself. God can, and most certainly will, direct my vote. I have noticed that a lot of the younger multicultural churches aren't playing by the old political religious rules of 'you must toe this line or else'. Those churches are following the teachings of Jesus, caring for the poor, concerning themselves with racial justice, and working on a form of 'all things common', which is the biblical practice described in Acts Chapter 2 verse 44, where those who had much, shared with those who didn't. Most of these churches as I've seen; are also multi-ethnic in leadership.

I admit that if I visit a new church, I look for diversity on the platform. Who is on the prayer team and the praise and worship team? I love diversity. I love people. I love different cultures, backgrounds, ethnicities, and food. I love to hear of the different experiences that people have in their neighborhoods, their countries, their lives. I come alive with that sort of thing, so when I see the singers or the leaders on the platform aren't a diverse group, I'll often wonder why.

There are many reasons and thus I ask the questions:

- Did other people groups not want to be included in the mix?
- If not, why?
- Did they take a look at the thirteen-page volunteer application form that included questions such as:

    - Your current job, your jobs for the last five years, social security number etc., and they suddenly changed their minds about volunteering?

- Did they go through the application process to volunteer their services, but their skills weren't what that church was looking for?
- Did they apply, have great skills, but were still rejected because they didn't have the look that the church wanted for their praise team?

THE HARDCORE EVANGELICAL

The Church has traditionally done business in a certain manner, so it's a challenge to get most churches to move out of the current mold in order to accommodate a new body of believers.

This new body of believers; also love Jesus and His Word but have no desire to worship from hymnals, tote a huge Bible to church, and raise money through selling chicken dinners. Most churches are stubborn to change, I call them the change resistors who believe that unless things stay as they always have been, some may not make it through the pearly gates of heaven. If someone describes themselves as hard core evangelical, I could get chills.

To me, the term hard-core evangelical usually means they are super religious, unloving, and unyielding. This harsh, hard, way of dealing with others in the church is driven by a demonic spirit of religion. In many ways organized religion is run very much like organized crime because there is a lot of oppression that is disguised as love, as well as heavy doses of control and manipulation.

Four years ago, I was talking to someone that I met while out running at Battery Park, and we discovered that we were both Christians. She asked me, *"Is your Church Democrat or Republican?"* I was surprised at the question because I didn't realize that was something a church should be! After I quickly scanned my mind for the answer, I became very happy that I didn't know the answer to that question!

I had never ever thought about my church in that way. My Pastor doesn't have time for that nonsense! He and his wife are busy teaching us about the Grace of God, the goodness of God, and how to develop a relationship with Jesus. So, is my church a Republican church? Or are we a Democratic church? I have no clue and I am so happy to say that! What I do know is that we are a Christian Church, saved by God's Grace, Jesus loves us, and we love Him!

What would it look like if we would choose to really get to know each other, choose to understand the road someone is currently walking on, and choose to know each other's story, rather than sitting back and pointing fingers? When we don't understand why people do the things they do, it's because we do not know or understand their story. Clearly the decisions they made were made because they acted on the information they had at that time. You and I have done the same! Maya Angelou said, *"When you know better, you do better."* But what do you do when you don't know better? You do what you know, and it doesn't always turn out right.

One of the reasons that describing ourselves as conservative evangelicals keeps us in a narrow place, is because it severely limits what extent and how often God can work through us to reach people. After all, isn't that what Christianity is all about? Reaching the dying world through the message of the Gospel of Grace? Our fights over doctrine will pale at the sight of Jesus because when He appears everyone will be looking to Him! We won't have the desire or the time to fight each other when Jesus shows up.

The same is true for fights between Republicans versus Democrats, Liberals versus Conservatives, Black people versus White people. At the sight of Jesus, every title given by man falls away, it simply melts in His presence.

So will all the bickering and fighting over things like which days we should worship, whether we should eat bacon or not, and whether we could sing on the praise team with cornrows. We are Christians!

How is it that we have adopted the names coined by the world, wear them as mantles, insist that this is the only narrow way to live; and then try to make it so that everyone around us should live this way, or else? This is narrow conservatism gone wild.

THE HAVE AND THE HAVE NOTS

If we could all agree that Jesus is Who we're modeling, preaching and becoming, that would be such a good start!

Instead, one church or camp believes that they have the declarations and confessions done correctly and that everyone else is wrong. Another camp believes that they have the correct day to worship correctly and everyone else worshipping on other days, are wrong.

One camp believes that speaking in other tongues is a must for every Christian, and yet another camp believes that speaking in other tongues has already passed away and everyone who speaks in other tongues has totally lost their minds or is hanging out with the devil. These are the things that have been preached from pulpits across the nation for decades.

It's a challenge to find the love of God in some churches because even though we preach consistently about the unconditional love of God, practicing that love outside of our camps is not as consistent as the preaching of it is. As a result of these highly emphasized differences, some congregations have begun to look at other congregations with the assertion of their opinion, that 'we have it right and you have it wrong'.

Even within one local body there are pronounced sub-divisions, one of which I call the haves and the have nots. You either have faith like we have, or you don't, you either pray the way we do, or else you're wrong. You either have it like we have it, or you're wrong. The haves and the have-nots... We have it, you don't.

This is how it works: If someone shows up at a church service not dressed 'properly,' or the car they're driving looks like it is held together by duct tape; or their tithes and offerings amount to several pennies in a plastic bag, then that is a clear indication to the rest of the congregation that the person isn't reading the Bible often enough, their relationship with Jesus is not up to par, and there is a spirit of disobedience somewhere in that person's life. That person is a have-not, and they are judged by how much stuff they do not have.

There are also other labels: Liberals versus Conservatives as well as Grace versus Religion. At this moment in time, we're at the point of the Black Christian church versus White Christian church which manifested partly because some of our leaders continued to uphold the racist rhetoric of the Trump administration without acknowledging the error of it to their congregations. That stance, coupled with the murder of George Floyd on May 25, 2020, has brought the Church to where we are today, which is a more divided state than we've ever been.

It's no fun to have to jump through all the hoops to be accepted at church. If I'm wearing jeans and you're in a fancy suit and high heels, then good for you! Maybe that's not what I feel like wearing today. Or, maybe I don't have, or want a fancy suit and high heels! Or maybe I'd like to have it but cannot afford it right now. Either way, shouldn't I still be allowed to worship alongside you and be accepted the way I am? The answer is yes, and in most cases, you're allowed to worship. Yet when it comes to being accepted by the church clique it's a hard no.

Acceptance is key because it makes us all one. When we take time out of our day to point out what someone is wearing or attempt to make them feel different or judged for not wearing what we're wearing; our witness is lost on that person.

For me that issue is personal, because one Sunday at the end of the service someone said to me, *"You don't ever wear Sunday church clothes, if you did, it would make you look so nice!"* That is so sad! How many people have we run out of our churches because we had an opinion about their clothes that we just couldn't help but share with them?

In case you're wondering, I did eventually leave that church after a year of absorbing some good teaching that unfortunately was mixed in with religion, political grandstanding, and public shaming of the then-president and his political party. I do not ever attend church to hear about politics, I attend so that I could be taught the Word of God.

POLITICAL GAIN

A major part of the great divide that has separated the body of Christ in the United States over a span of five years has had to do with the strong conservative stand evangelicals took in supporting President Trump.

As we took that stand, several church leaders (as they do every election season) urged, coaxed, and in some cases tried to manipulate their congregations to only vote for conservative candidates because the Republican platform best describes the values of the Church, and the values of Jesus.

As a result, several million Christian voters turned out en masse, to support the Republican platform, some because they believed that they were in essence voting for the platform and not the person or the party, and some believed that they were following the leading of the Holy Spirit, and some believed that 'as long as Pastor said it', it came directly from heaven. Lately, I've been viewing the evangelical Church as a political entity.

And to a certain extent, I have stopped evaluating us based on spirituality. For some churches there is no longer even a pretense of following the teachings of Jesus, some just make up their messages as they go along, completely laying the Holy Spirit to the side even though He lives on the inside to help us with just that.

At times I've wondered: those that carry the conservative evangelical name as a badge of honor, are they just a group of religious people, much like those who crucified Christ, except this group has a couple of Bibles in different translations? In essence, they've now become their own Political Action Committee.

As the world (and some of the Church) watch the massive scoops of hypocrisy served up in church services every weekend, and as we observe Pastors as they ignore issues facing the communities in which the church building stands, and the greater dedication paid to politics rather than Christianity, it seems as though some congregations are being used for political gain, publicity and financing.

John 3:16
King James Version (KJV)

[16] For God so loved the world, that he gave his only begotten Son, that whosoever believeth in him should not perish, but have everlasting life.

John Chapter 3 verse 16 shows us that God doesn't just love America, but the whole world. At times, the evangelical arm of Christianity seems to be a movement that revels in condemning the poor, immigrants, the LGBTQ community, people of color, and everyone else who does not line up with the picture in their minds of what their brand of evangelicalism should look like.

LET THE HOLY GHOST LEAD

If we introduce people to Jesus by presenting the Gospel to them, the only other thing to do is to stand back and allow the Holy Spirit to take them in the direction that He chooses.

We don't need to add anything else to their experience. Some of what is taught to us about the Word of God comes from the experiences of church leaders rather than what the Bible really says.

So now there's a confused Church going to God saying:

"Well Pastor so-and-so says that we should do it this way, and then we can take Communion. Prophet this-and-that said that we should be sure to always have our scriptures written out, and we must have no less than 3 scriptures so that this thing can happen."

Did God say any of that? He probably did! Yet when he did, He wasn't talking to you, He was talking to Pastor so-and-so, and Prophet this-and-that, the person to whom He gave the information in the first place. He spoke it that way for them because God knows exactly what their learning style is and what they need to do in order to get themselves in position to receive what He has for them.

Pastor so-and-so or Prophet this-and-that, then passed that information on to you, me and all the other congregants; and it quickly became doctrine in the Church even though it wasn't meant for everyone.

That's one of the reasons why on many occasions, there has been no manifestation of answered prayer in our lives because we're acting on instructions God gave to someone else. Those instructions and those directions were never meant for me or you. What if the prophetic words that we receive from church leadership came with the blue check mark that is used by social media giants, Twitter, Instagram, and Facebook to verify authenticity?

When we see that mark on a social media post, we know that the person posting has been verified by the management of that particular social media platform, and that the tweets and posts have actually come from the person whose name is on the social media account, or someone from their team; right?

So, we know it's legit! Just think about it...When a word of prophecy comes from a leader and that word was meant for them personally, then misunderstood and in turn given as doctrine to the entire congregation; we would all know not to pay attention to what was said to us if the blue checkmark wasn't present.

If the blue verification checkmark was present, it would mean that this word came from God and it is meant for the entire congregation, not just a personal word for the leader. Of course, that's just my wishful thinking because we all have the Spirit of God living in us, and He is the One Who leads and guides us. It is still a nice thought though, but even without man's verifications God shows us what is for us and what is not, in His own way!

THE PROPHETIC VOICE

It's this same narrow way of thinking that causes conservative evangelicals to receive prophetic words directly from heaven, yet it's distributed/interpreted through a narrowed conservative lens. Therefore, it's reserved only for specific conservative candidates during the election cycle.

That same narrow spirit, if it ever has a word for someone that isn't of the conservative persuasion, will give a word that is harsh, with an ultimatum at the end. This is what makes some Holy-Spirit-led congregations think: Is this Prophet truly hearing God or not? The same narrow spirit also has words from heaven for their congregation, the ones that they know personally sitting in the first three rows; the ones who sometimes have their names on the seats. The ones whose personal business the Pastor already knows.

This narrow spirit calls the person out by name, refers to a personal situation in that person's life and begins to prophesy directly to that person, speaking the thing that the person has already told them about. The person receiving the word nods excitedly at receiving this word from the Lord, but most of the congregation isn't fooled. The Pastor is prophesying to his friend, and he already knows his friend's business.

Am I saying that God doesn't give prophetic words **to** friends **for** friends? **No**. I am saying that it would be nice to see prophetic words given to someone sitting all the way in the back, someone you've never seen before. Give that person a word that resonates with their spirit and brings peace to his/her mind. My Bible tells me that the gifts of the Spirit are divided to every man, given by the Holy Spirit as He wills!

1 Corinthians 12:11
King James Version (KJV)

[11] But all these worketh that one and the selfsame Spirit, dividing to every man severally as he will.

This is different than hearing a word that doesn't come to pass in the time that we think it should, or in the time that we were told it would. It's when we add dates and times (out of our humanness) to prophetic words that things get confusing.

Sometimes God speaks to a Prophet, and when the Prophet says it to the congregation, we then get excited and we repeat it, we declare it, we confess it, and we pray it. *"God said blah, blah, will happen this summer."* Well, maybe He did say blah and blah and in the human excitement of the news, the Prophet added a date and time: *"by this summer."*

That's when things get messy, because we're all expecting it to happen by this summer! Yet Summer comes and goes, then Fall, Winter, eventually Spring comes and goes by without us seeing physical proof or manifestation of what the Prophet said.

The following year, here comes summer again and guess what? Wait a minute! *"Maybe Prophet so-and-so meant* ***this*** *summer, not* ***last*** *summer!* ***OMG!*** *Come on everybody, grab the prophetic word and let's believe again!"* And so, the demonic cycle continues.

There have been words of prophecy that were spoken fifty, seventy, even a hundred years ago that are just now coming to pass in 2021. That's different. That's how the prophetic works. It was prophesied that Jesus would come to earth eons before it happened.

How would it have looked if God had declared that Jesus would be born in the year 1619, and it didn't happen? Well, the answer is this: If God said that Jesus was going to be born in 1619, it would have happened then. Whatever God says, comes to pass. It always does, and that's the key to hearing and receiving prophecy. If it's God, it will come to pass.

COVID-19 IN THE EVANGELICAL CHURCH

Touch your neighbor if you remember when many in the Church touted that the AIDS epidemic of the 90's was sent by God as punishment. (I understand some reading this book right now still feel the same way.) Now here we are with the same item on the

Church's healing agenda; that the Coronavirus was also sent from God as punishment for disobedience. I hope your church isn't teaching you that, thank God mine isn't.

When New York City was being ravaged by the Coronavirus in the Spring and Summer of 2020, I was told by someone that I should leave New York and relocate to Texas because New York City had no respect for President Trump, that we were a 'blue state', and that the hand of God would never intervene to help the state of New York with the virus.

Then four months later, the great state of Texas became the first state to surpass one million Coronavirus cases. How could that be? Red state = God's hands of protection *is* available. Blue state = God's hands of protection **is not** available.

Yet this red state with the hand of God's protection on it, was in the throes of the pandemic in the same way as New York City (blue state) was!

WHICH IS IT REALLY?

What did the great state of Texas do now, to get God angry? Can we see how dangerous that way of thinking/teaching is? It's amazing that we have found yet another area to create division. The

Coronavirus, is it real or not? Should we use masks or not? Should we forsake assembling or not?

Then one camp had to let the other camp know that the first camp trusted in God, the Blood of Jesus, Psalms 91, and they had faith. The other camp responded with: *"You don't love your neighbor if you don't wear a mask."* My God!

Think of how different it would be if we never had labels in the first place, if labels never took the place of Jesus. We would be focused on Jesus and whether someone wanted to wear a mask or not they wouldn't be judged, they would be loved, enabling the healing power of God to flow!

Who knew that in 2020 and 2021 the Church would be even more divided because of a virus? Who knew that the great falling away could come because of whether we wear masks or not?

Or whether we took the Covid-19 shot or not? This was the perfect time for us to unite in healing our nation, but it didn't happen.

We don't need the God-kind of faith to make intelligent decisions; we just need to unconditionally love everyone we come into contact with. At the time of this writing, to mask or not to mask, and to vaccinate or not vaccinate have now become additional tools of division in the body of Christ.

One thing is for sure: The Church didn't know what to do with Covid-19 and that's because we were not united against it; we spent that time fighting about masks, whether we should attend church services or not and deciding who had faith based on whether or not they received the Covid-19 vaccination.

Even if you turned your television off, stayed off social media and never surfed the internet, I can still guarantee that you know at least one person who was either infected with, or died from the Coronavirus.

The facts are that the Coronavirus seemed to be everywhere! However, the truth is that you and I have already been healed by the stripes of Jesus as stated in the Book of Isaiah Chapter 53 verses 3-5.

Isaiah 53:3-5
King James Version (KJV)

[3] He is despised and rejected of men; a man of sorrows, and acquainted with grief: and we hid as it were our faces from him; he was despised, and we esteemed him not.

[4] Surely he hath borne our griefs, and carried our sorrows: yet we did esteem him stricken, smitten of God, and afflicted.

[5] But he was wounded for our transgressions, he was bruised for our iniquities: the chastisement of our peace was upon him; and with his stripes we are healed.

Because of the truth of God's Word that we were healed by His stripes, is it now okay for churches to still gather for Sunday service in spite of city and state officials asking their residents to wear masks and practice social distancing? Is it that we're desperate to fellowship with each other because we haven't seen each other physically since March 2020 and we miss each other? Or is it that we think that if people don't show up for church services right now, the finances of the local church will drop, and membership levels will plummet?

Or is it because the Holy Spirit told your local church leadership to go ahead and open the church? I'm not sure which it was, but I do know that large numbers of churchgoers have been infected and many have died because of the virus. May they rest in peace and in power.

The Coronavirus came in somewhat like a hurricane and took most of the Church by surprise. As of November 2021, according to the Centers for

Disease Control and Prevention, there have been 46.4 million cases and 754,000 deaths in the United States.

Maybe you've had the virus, maybe you know someone who died from it, or maybe you believe it's a hoax and someone is making up all these viruses and numbers. Either way, I want you to know that if you've had the virus or if you lost someone to the virus, I send my love and condolences to you and to your family.

I didn't think I'd see the day when the faith of a believer was reduced to, *'If you have faith, you don't need a mask'*. I understand that thought pattern, but it seems like maybe some of the same people who won't wear a mask because they have faith and because Jesus' Blood will protect them, are the same ones who also wear seatbelts when they drive, and the same ones who want to purchase extra guns to protect themselves.

This doesn't need to be so complicated. We can no longer take every available excuse to widen the division in the body of Christ. Are we really causing more divisions now because of a mask?

If we believe that wearing a mask will help to protect us and others, then those that don't believe the same way shouldn't be accused of being heartless. Choosing not to wear a mask is no indication of whether someone has faith or not! I saw a social media post where someone complained about wearing a mask and said it was 'so oppressive'. Listen!

Centuries of lynching, enslavement, murder, discrimination, and mass incarceration of Black people - that is oppression. But when you are required to wear a mask during a global pandemic… That is **not** oppression. How privileged is your life when wearing a mask is the most oppressed you've ever felt?

With the negative effects of the Corona virus there also must be a plan for abolishing poverty and a plan to drastically reduce the socio-economic gap; that starts within the Church. Black people and people of color sitting in our congregations are not only being disproportionately killed by the pandemic but are being disproportionately impacted by the economic downturn as a result of the pandemic as well. Dr Martin Luther King Jr. once said that racial injustice and economic injustice are "inseparable twins."

Chapter 3

COGNITIVE DISSONANCE

HIGHLIGHTING BLACK WOMEN:

BREONNA TAYLOR *was a 26-year-old woman who was shot multiple times in her home in Louisville, Kentucky when police officers forced entry as part of an investigation into drug-dealing operations. Her wounds were fatal. The police later realized that they were at the wrong house; no one has been charged with her murder. Rest in peace and power, Breonna!*

A dictionary meaning of Cognitive Dissonance is: *The mental stress or discomfort experienced by a person who simultaneously holds two or more contradictory beliefs, ideas or values; when performing an action that contradicts one of those beliefs, ideas, or values; or when confronted with new information that contradicts one of the beliefs, ideas, and values.*

Sometimes in our minds we can hold a core belief that is extremely strong, and when we are presented with evidence that works against the already rooted core belief, that new evidence cannot be accepted.

We then begin to experience mental discomfort, confusion, and the inability to understand present situations. The intense discomfort of the mind is called Cognitive Dissonance. The mind, as it tries to cover over that core, rooted belief, will refute, avoid, and deny anything that doesn't fit into the space with the strong core belief, even if that strong core belief is wrong.

I didn't realize it, but I was experiencing Cognitive Dissonance for several years. As a born-again Christian, being introduced to confessions and declarations was a part of my life. I saw and heard my Pastors do it, they encouraged us to do it, and so I did. However, they got results, I didn't. I thought it was my fault maybe I had done something, or several things wrong. They were doing it right I was doing it wrong. That's why they got results, but I didn't. As I continued learning and growing in Faith (which took more than a couple of years), I discovered that I was not the only one experiencing difficulties and delays in getting results.

I also was not the only one experiencing the mental anguish that accompanied such behavior with our own eyes, created mental and physical stress in our lives at levels we had never anticipated, or expected to experience. However, we all felt that we were the ones doing something wrong. We heard from several leaders in the church that if we weren't getting results it was because we either weren't tithing, or we needed to be serving in an area of ministry (volunteering to work with the children, singing in the choir, going into prisons and nursing homes etc.) or that we were not confessing enough of the scriptures. I was confused. Confusion is the key in the Cognitive Dissonance experience.

There were several Christians that I personally knew who were experiencing the same Cognitive Dissonance. The dissonance between what we were told by our spiritual leaders - that had now taken root in us, and what we saw. I couldn't figure out why there were no results in my life because I was doing all of what I was told to do! I was jumping, quite expertly I might add, through all the evangelical hoops!

One night, after several years of this mental confusion and dissonance I was sitting at church, and my Pastor told the congregation that if we didn't tithe, we would be placed back under the curse of the law, and that the devourer would not be rebuked in our lives anymore because we would have 'tied the hands of God'.

The devourer is Satan, the enemy of the Church so I sat there thinking that the devil now had free reign over my life and the lives of my children and there was nothing I could do about it, except to give the 10 percent to my local church, and go back and count all the times I didn't tithe and multiply that by 20% (which was a common teaching at that time), and give it all to my church. Help me Lord!

Normally whenever I heard something along those lines I would sit and reason: *"My God what now? What new thing should I be doing, or what was I doing wrong? What did I now need to fix or change?"* This wasn't the first time I'd heard something like that, but on this particular night, for some blessed reason, I heard it in a different way.

I suddenly knew that my Pastor was wrong! After I heard the Pastor's words, a quiet, peaceful thought entered my mind, and I whispered it to my girlfriend sitting next to me: *"If Jesus Christ has already redeemed me from the curse of the law, who on earth has the ability to place me back under the curse? Who is that strong to undo what Jesus did?"* Certainly not the person standing in the pulpit, or anyone else!

We both looked at each other with narrowed eyes, thinking: *"Oh my goodness, what we had believed for so long was a lie!"* There was clearly some reason we weren't receiving results, and it had nothing to do with us not being regular tithers, nor the devourer capturing us, because at that point in time we both were tithing. It had nothing to do with us not volunteering our time, because we both were.

I had all the things on the evangelical checklist checked off, and I was proud of it too! I'll be the first one to wave a hand and say that I was not a regular tither in the early days.

I remember once, back in the 90's after I got my paycheck but couldn't pay all the bills, still needing food, pampers, and gas, standing in my kitchen saying: *"You know what Jesus? I love you I really do, but I also need food, I need pampers, and I need gas. I also need to pay Daisy (the babysitter). So, I'm not going to be tithing this week, and I probably won't be able to do it next week either. But I do love you!"* Guess what?

God didn't strike me dead. He didn't place me back under the curse to learn a hard lesson. He didn't send the devourer after me. He didn't even get mad. What I had been hearing was all a lie, although at the time I didn't know that.

I just thought: Well, I'm taking a chance here by not tithing, because if I don't pay the babysitter, she won't keep the baby, then I won't be able to go to work, then I won't have a paycheck, which means I won't have food, or gas, or pampers, and we would be thrown out of our apartment.

I didn't factor in the Grace of God or the love of God. In fact, I knew very little about that at that time. Let me help you before you begin to think: *"Sherma you should have read the Bible for yourself, and you would have seen that what you were hearing was wrong."*

The thing is, most people tend to read their Bibles and hear what is being said to them, in the vein, in the thought space, in the mental arenas, and sometimes even in the voice, of their Pastors, (or whoever has been teaching them the Word of God most frequently).

As you sit at church listening to a message being preached, that message, and everything in it, hits your mind as a seed that is planted. If you purchase the CD of that sermon, or download it, and keep on listening to it, that seed drops into your spirit and is now a part of you, the seed has sprouted and is beginning to grow in you.

Pretty soon, you will believe that way, think that way, speak that way, and yes, at times, it's possible that you will hear God that way too, (the way you've been taught).

Except, **that way** could be wrong. Jesus left us with His Holy Spirit to live in us, lead and guide us, and to help us as we read and study the Bible. In many cases though, we end up learning how to be led by our church leadership, rather than by being led by God's Spirit, and therein lies the problem. Folks, the devourer has already been devoured.

Jesus Himself took care of that. Jesus Himself destroyed the works of the devil. Jesus Himself disarmed principalities and powers for our sake!

The devourer that you're being reminded of at church, on Sundays and on Wednesdays just before the offering is taken… He has already been eternally defeated and you and I have authority over him, ha!

1 John 3:8
New King James Version (NKJV)

[8] He who sins is of the devil, for the devil has sinned from the beginning. For this purpose, the Son of God was manifested, that He might destroy the works of the devil.

Colossians 2:15-17
Amplified Bible, Classic Edition (AMPC)

[15][God] disarmed the principalities and powers that were ranged against us and made a bold display *and* public example of them, in triumphing over them in Him *and* in it [the cross].

What I had been experiencing throughout all those years was Cognitive Dissonance! The extreme mental distress, the conflicting thoughts in my mind about receiving results was Cognitive Dissonance! Hearing one thing, expecting to see what I'd heard, but not seeing anything remotely close.

Even when I was confronted with new information that clearly showed me that what I had believed for so long; wasn't true, I couldn't come to terms with it! I refused to believe it and pushed the thoughts away. I never even realized that it was the Holy Spirit trying to give me a way out and a peaceful resolution. I thought it was the devourer (who had already been devoured but I was way too stressed to figure that one out!)

Like everyone else though, I continued to faithfully show up at church, and I continued to volunteer. I continued visiting the prisons (I loved volunteering with that ministry because the transparency and love of the leaders of the Prison Ministry made things so much better!).

On my own, my daughter and I volunteered at one of the homeless shelters in our city, and I also for a good while, helped with the Food Bank. I kept myself busy with works, and I loved doing it.

Through all of it I knew that I was not the only one just going through the motions, saying and doing one thing and expecting a certain result, yet never seeing any of the results I thought I would receive. Year after year, those results never manifested and even though

I knew I should be doing something different about it, I stayed with it because I was encouraged to.

I just knew that one day things would change and manifest and everything would be just as I was told. My grandmother used to say: *"One day, one day, congotay!"* What that means is that one day everyone must pay for their misdeeds. Except in this situation, the one that seemed to be paying, through Cognitive Dissonance, was me.

One would think that the mental distress (or dissonance) that I was experiencing would have forced me to take different steps, forced me to try to find a way out, but I really believed at that time, that what I was doing was right, and of course there were many scriptures to back up what I had been taught.

I didn't have the wisdom back then to understand that those Old Testament scriptures weren't even written for me to practice in this dispensation, and that I was under the dispensation of Grace.

I read it in the scriptures sure, but I kept remembering Malachi 3:9 that said I was cursed with a curse because I was robbing God. I knew that even though I wasn't robbing God in that present season, I had robbed Him in the past, so I figured that my *'one day, one day, congotay'* moment had arrived. All I could do was sweat it out and pay my dues, because one day soon, it would all be better.

At the beginning of every year, there would be all these different prophetic words that came from different leaders in the Church, prophesying what type of year we would have. Every year I thought the same thing:

The prophetic word for (whatever the year was) is for me! I'm going to confess it and it will come to pass for me, manifestation is coming my way for sure this year! Every single year at our annual meetings or convocations I just knew that there would be something different that would happen, and I would finally see what I had believed God for.

What really happened however, was that every year at our annual meeting, there were not a whole lot of manifestations (for me), but I still wouldn't miss a single meeting! I'd be there with a bag packed with sandwiches, juice, water bottles, and snacks, as I went through the same scenario… Year after year.

What to do?

Romans 15:4
Amplified Bible, Classic Edition
(AMPC)

"For whatever was thus written in former days was written for our instruction, that by [our steadfast and patient] endurance and the encouragement [drawn] from the Scriptures, we might hold fast to and cherish hope."

The Old Testament scriptures were given to us so that we could learn from the different stories and situations that were experienced. We could read first-hand of their trials and tribulations, and how they overcame them. We read about their mistakes and their triumphs, their sins, and consequences.

We also saw how God brought them out of seemingly impossible situations. I could clearly see now how different things were under the dispensation of Grace that we now live in. At the time I didn't see it that way though. I was caught up in the cycle of 'Ten ways to be Blessed', 'Five Steps to Prosperity', and 'What to do if your Faith doesn't work,' sermons.

I simply continued to spin. Cognitive Dissonance had me in its grip, but even though I didn't realize it at the time, somewhere in the back of my mind I had begun to think that there was a lot that needed to change. Something, somewhere, was definitely wrong and I am so thankful that the Holy Spirit eventually brought me out of Cognitive Dissonance with His Word and by helping me to develop an intimate relationship with Him.

THE SHEEP AND THE GOATS

There is something else that I've thought about off and on over the years. It has to do with the spirit of fear in the Church about the United States becoming a 'goat nation' if we didn't do right by the nation of Israel. I heard what sounded like fear coming from pulpits, where leaders were saying that if our government (democratic at the time) made the wrong move concerning Israel, the United States would be relegated to goat nation status.

What in the name of all the goats in the world is that about? Well, it's fear.

Fear loves when we don't rightly divide the Word of God because then it creeps in and brings more fear. Fear will keep us trapped in a box with Cognitive

Dissonance - believing what we heard from the pulpit, even though we could clearly see from the scriptures that what we were reading was different to what we had been hearing from the pulpit. We still chose to believe what we heard instead, even though it was a lie. Cognitive Dissonance was keeping us in its deceptive grip and slowly tightening its noose on our spiritual lives in that area. This is what the scripture says, check it out for yourself in Matthew 25:31-43 in the Message translation:

> **31-33 "When he finally arrives, blazing in beauty and all his angels with him, the Son of Man will take his place on his glorious throne. Then all the nations will be arranged before him and he will sort the people out, much as a shepherd sorts out sheep and goats, putting sheep to his right and goats to his left.**
>
> **34-36 "Then the King will say to those on his right, 'Enter, you who are blessed by my Father! Take what's coming to you in this kingdom. It's been ready for you since the world's foundation.**
>
> **And here's why:**
>
> **I was hungry and you fed me,**
> **I was thirsty and you gave me a drink,**
> **I was homeless and you gave me a room,**
> **I was shivering and you gave me clothes,**
> **I was sick and you stopped to visit,**
> **I was in prison and you came to me.'**

[37-40] "Then those 'sheep' are going to say, 'Master, what are you talking about? When did we ever see you hungry and feed you, thirsty and give you a drink? And when did we ever see you sick or in prison and come to you?' Then the King will say, 'I'm telling the solemn truth: Whenever you did one of these things to someone overlooked or ignored, that was me—you did it to me.'

[41-43] "Then he will turn to the 'goats,' the ones on his left, and say, 'Get out, worthless goats! You're good for nothing but the fires of hell. And why? Because—

I was hungry and you gave me no meal,
I was thirsty and you gave me no drink,
I was homeless and you gave me no bed,
I was shivering and you gave me no clothes,
Sick and in prison, and you never visited.'

[44] "Then those 'goats' are going to say, 'Master, what are you talking about? When did we ever see you hungry or thirsty or homeless or shivering or sick or in prison and didn't help?

45 "He will answer them, 'I'm telling the solemn truth: Whenever you failed to do one of these things to someone who was being overlooked or ignored, that was me—you failed to do it to me.'

Verse 32 in the King James Version (KJV) says:

"And before Him shall be gathered all nations: and He shall separate them one from another, as a shepherd divideth his sheep from the goats:"

Based on the above, we see that goat nations refer to those (people or nations) who didn't feed the hungry, clothe the naked, take in the stranger and visit those who are in prison. That certainly puts a whole different spin on things, doesn't it?

Especially when you consider it in light of what's going on with minorities, immigrants at America's borders, injustice and inequality.

Cognitive Dissonance is unable to make room for new information when it is presented to us, it continues to hold on to the previous information even without proof or manifestation, never considering the possibility that maybe something different should be done to produce results!

This is why it is so dangerous, because it keeps us living in the land of *'I-don't-know-why-this-isn't-*

working-but-I'll-do-it-until-it-works'. Then, thirty years later we look up and we're still in the same place, doing the same thing, nothing much has worked, and we begin to blame God. Albert Einstein has been credited with saying that the definition of insanity is doing the same thing over and over again while expecting different results. Something must change, else some in the body of Christ who were/are in a position like I was, will remain in a state of mind where they're unable to be their real selves.

Cognitive Dissonance causes masks to appear and most of the Church is known for the masks that we wear to face each other as well as to face the world. The world isn't buying it though, not even for a minute because they too are clamoring for authenticity, they want more of the real. It's challenging to find authentic people nowadays, when even reality TV is being scripted.

JUMP!

If you are reading this book and you are thinking that what you've been experiencing is Cognitive Dissonance, please do yourself (and me) a favor and get off the hamster wheel right away. Get out of the religious rat race right now. It isn't doing you any good, and you'll save yourself a load of mental distress and discouragement. The thing about the hamster wheel is that it never ever stops for you to get off. You're going to have to jump off while the wheels are still turning.

Based on what you've read in this chapter, you're going to have to take a leap of faith and decide that you will no longer be a passenger on the Cognitive Dissonance train. The Holy Spirit wants to help you to get off; He has been working tirelessly to get you to jump off the train of religion and dissonance. Like me, you've probably been holding on to your beliefs, unwilling (and unable) to let go of the wrong thinking.

The time has come, it's your time to take that leap of faith and jump into His waiting arms, say goodbye to Cognitive Dissonance! After you take that leap, make another quality decision to spend as much time as you can, working on your relationship with Jesus by spending time reading and understanding the Word of God. It will become simpler and easier to be led by His Spirit as you do that. His Spirit within you will show you what you need to do next, and what ministry (if any) to volunteer your services, where to apply for a job, who to marry, how to vote, where to live, and other things pertaining to your life.

The thing that saved me in the middle of the dissonance was that I kept on reading the Word of God, I kept up with the studying of it. I could read the Bible and pray for hours on end, and not take a breather. Even now it still is my favorite thing to do, it still gets me energized, yet keeps me in a place of peace.

I mentioned in Chapter 2 that the Word of Faith camp, instilled in me the importance of the Word of God. I heard one of the leaders suggest that we begin reading some of the Bible every day for thirty days just to see if life would change. Well, I started reading a little every day, and never even noticed when the thirty days went by, I enjoyed it so much!

WALKING OUT OF COGNITIVE DISSONANCE

I realized that what I was experiencing was Cognitive Dissonance as I was in prayer one day and those two words came up in my Spirit: Cognitive Dissonance.

I scribbled it in my prayer journal and didn't think it had anything to do with me, because it came up as I was praying (or so I thought) over someone else. (That is something else I learned as I stayed with the Word of God and prayer, is that I should always pay attention while I'm praying, and not let my mind run all over New York City.

I need to **pray** in the Spirit, and **stay** in the Spirit while I'm praying, so that the 'arm of flesh', my fleshy tendencies, don't come in and take a seat, thereby distorting what I've heard in the Spirit realm, and deceiving my mind). The arm of the flesh refers to a Bible Passage where the King of Assyria came up with a multitude of people against King Hezekiah, and King Hezekiah comforted his people with these words:

2 Chronicles 32:8
King James Version (KJV)

[8] With him is an arm of flesh; but with us is the LORD our God to help us, and to fight our battles. And the people rested themselves upon the words of Hezekiah king of Judah.

So, I ignored the two words *'Cognitive Dissonance,'* until a couple of days later, those same two words popped back up in my prayer time and this time I was praying over a different matter! Then there was yet another occasion that those two words popped back up in prayer, making it three times now, on three different occasions, as I was praying over three different things!

I looked back in my prayer journal and realized that the only thing that was common, on the three occasions I'd heard those words, was me! I began to earnestly pray over it. I also searched for the dictionary meaning and googled references. Little by little, the Holy Spirit began to show me where the traps were, how I had been caught, and what I needed to do in order to get out.

All I had to do was agree with the Holy Spirit that I needed to change and that I was willing to do whatever He showed me to do. I also made an agreement with my own self, that I knew that something was wrong, something needed fixing and that whatever the changes were, no matter how hard they were to make, I would be 100% obedient to the leading of the Holy Spirit.

Day by day, the Holy Spirit took me through various scriptures, He showed me what I'd been taught at church and how it had been interpreted, versus what He said and meant in His Word. I admit that most of it was very difficult to let go of. There even was a period of time where I doubted that I was even hearing from the Holy Spirit Himself! I thought: *'This is so painful to let go, why would the Holy Spirit want to do that to me, why would he want to cause me mental pain and anguish? Surely this can't be God, this is the devil for sure!'*

One instance that comes to mind right now is the idea that if I tolerate even an ounce of fear in my life, it will completely contaminate my faith. I believed this for so very long that now as the Holy Spirit was enlightening me with His Word, showing me how wrong that teaching was. I doubted that it was Him doing the enlightening! This Cognitive Dissonance is no joke! We're born again of incorruptible seed (1 Peter 1:23) and incorruptible seed cannot produce fruit that corrupts. Incorruptible fruit is the fruit that is produced by incorruptible seed. This is seed which cannot ever be corrupted. So, if faith comes from hearing the Word (Romans 10:17) and the Word is God (John 1:1), then my faith came from hearing God, right? God has dealt to every man the measure of faith (Romans 12:3).

God cannot give me anything that is able to be corrupted; where would God go to find faith that is able to be corrupted? Where would He find faith that is able to be contaminated or tainted? God isn't in the business of dealing with anything that can be tainted or corrupted, but I wasn't able to see that. I just believed what I had heard for so long. That, my friend, is the power of Cognitive Dissonance.

Here I was, in the throes of Cognitive Dissonance, prompted by the Holy Spirit to take a leap of faith. I had the Word of God to fall back on but didn't realize it at the time. The Word of God has always been and will always be a safe, gentle landing place. You will land there too.

Even if you feel like you don't have enough of the Word of God in you, that won't hinder Jesus. He Himself is the Word that you will be falling back on!

When you make the switch and jump off the religious Ferris wheel, all you must do is become preoccupied with Jesus and with His Word. When you do, I guarantee that you'll realize like I eventually did, **that receiving from God comes out of your relationship with Him and nothing else**. You can safely throw out all the gimmicks and prayer formulas. Get to know Jesus instead; you're really going to love all the changes He brings into your life!

You're going to have such a fun time as you receive revelation after revelation of the scriptures like you've never had before! Go read it for yourself, see that when Malachi Chapter 3:8-12 talks about bringing the tithe to the storehouse so that you wouldn't be cursed, that this was before Jesus came to redeem us from the curse. Allow the Holy Spirit to maneuver you through the Word showing you Grace versus the law.

If you are born again, you are already redeemed from the curse of the law! There's no more curse coming to get you! Sin has consequences, but because of Jesus' sacrifice we have been redeemed and forgiven of all our sins. All means all. The sins of the past, the present and the future, all forgiven! Grace will always be there to pick us up when we fall, so please don't allow yourself to be manipulated by gimmicks, and don't give under compulsion either!

2 Corinthians 9:7
Amplified Bible, Classic Edition (AMPC)

[7] Let each one [give] as he has made up his own mind *and* purposed in his heart, not reluctantly *or* sorrowfully or under compulsion, for God loves (He takes pleasure in, prizes above other things, and is unwilling to abandon or to do without) a cheerful (joyous, "prompt to do it") giver [whose heart is in his giving].

When you realize that what you've been hearing isn't true, or right, you'll begin to experience a freedom and a joy that has been missing in your life that you didn't even realize was missing! I encourage you to examine what you've heard in the past, in light of what's working and what's not working in your life.

Sit with the Holy Spirit in your quiet time and allow Him to expose all the lies you've been taught. I am totally convinced that most of the Bible teachers we had didn't deliberately set out to deceive us. They were trying their best to help us and teach us even though some of what they were teaching us was wrong. I once heard a Pastor explain it like this:

"Somebody taught it to somebody, who taught it to somebody else, and then that somebody else taught us. But the first somebody - was wrong." Now we're all wrong. Thankfully, the Holy Spirit has come to rescue us, He makes it all right!

LOGICAL LIVING

Many Christians have been living out of logic rather than by the leading of the Holy Spirit. There's nothing wrong with logic as long as we're not letting it rule our lives.

If we get with God for ourselves and allow the indwelling Holy Spirit to reveal Himself to us, our lives could become so much easier, and He will teach us how to make better choices. Sometimes there really is not a direct relationship between the choices we've made and what we're going through.

Sometimes things happen because there's a devil in the earth that is out to steal, to kill, and to destroy. Many times, that isn't what's been taught, so we blame ourselves every time something goes wrong.

For sure, we are to take stock of our lives; however, if every time something is wrong, we begin to heap condemnation on ourselves; that will send us deeper into a place of depression. Cognitive Dissonance can at times be wild beyond imagination because what it does is that it disables one's ability to make use of logic and reason.

Even though we're not led by logic, we do understand that logic as a course of thought helps us in various areas of life. Cognitive Dissonance locks the mind into a space where deception lives. As a result, we end up making decisions based on the deception and lies that we hold dear without allowing logic, reason, or even common sense to have a say, and without making room for the guidance of the Holy Spirit.

It seems that we've almost lost our souls as we continue covering up the things that we have no explanations for. This is what Cognitive Dissonance does. If we have belief systems that have been hacked by hearing and believing lies, then our intentions and our actions will also be hijacked by the same devil that hacked our belief systems in the first place!

We will end up holding on to the deception as though it's the last communion wafer in the pack while simultaneously ignoring the leading of the Holy Spirit. This is also another form of narrow religious conservatism because of the deception involved, and what it does to our lives. Believing a lie affects everything we do and say because it's challenging to try to reason with that kind of delusional thinking.

Others who are on the outside looking in and have recognized what is happening, often ignore the deceptive behavior because they don't want to have to deal with the delusion.

Anyone challenging the person being deceived ends up being on the messy end of the stick because the deceived person doesn't realize they're being deceived, and so they're unable to receive direction, correction or instruction. That's the nature of deception, you don't know that you're deceived.

Another area of deception pops up when there's cherry-picking of specific Bible passages to fit personal agendas, and the entire congregation gets caught up in the wrongly divided Word of God. However, real life experience has shown me that I need to have a personal relationship with God, and that is what has gotten me out of every rut.

No number of confessions, quoting scriptures aloud, taking communion every day, giving money to my Pastor, tithing regularly, joining the choir, working with the toddlers and praying without ceasing has done for me, what a solid relationship with Jesus Christ has done. I keep working on that relationship every chance I get!

Forming that solid relationship with Jesus has come from making time daily for Him. Yes, it's a challenge, given the busyness of life, but God comes first. He always comes first! Sometimes it's a rushed thirty minutes in the morning, but more often than not, it's a longer period of time. The key is to just work with the time that you have making sure to build your life around your time with Him, rather than trying to squeeze Jesus into a part of your day.

We are all a work in progress and when it comes to our relationship with Jesus; that is also a work in progress. What I want is for my relationship with Jesus tomorrow to be better than what I have with him today. Grace will lead us into that place, we simply have to let Him lead.

Chapter 4

THE EVANGELICAL VOTE

HIGHLIGHTING BLACK WOMEN:

<u>*TANISHA ANDERSON*</u> *was a 37-year-old woman who was killed after her family called 911 because Tanisha was having a mental health episode. The Medical Examiner ruled her death a homicide from 'sudden death associated with physical restraint in a prone position'. The police officer received a 10-day suspension. Rest in peace and power, Tanisha!*

If you were one of those, brave enough not to choose and accept the Republican party and you said it out loud, you probably were inundated with explanations of why you were wrong, and what your Republican vote could do for the Church, the Pro-Life platform, and for Israel.

Prepare yourself for the spirit of fear that produces guilt to show up and attempt to badger your mind about how great America will be again; and how much that will help Christianity around the world.

As some churches promote their Republican Jesus and read their Republican Bibles as they wrongly divide the Word of Truth, developing a close relationship with Jesus is not always on the agenda. This practice has been going on for decades while the Church has held on to the deceptive and ungodly narrative that God is only on one political side and not the other.

This is divisive and theologically incorrect. When the 2016 election rolled around, the division that was partially shoved under the carpets of most churches became even wider. It is the proverbial elephant in the sanctuary that most Christian leaders either don't know how to address, don't care enough to address it, or don't think that it matters. Except it does matter.

Many churches are split right down the middle: Democrat or Republican. Then depending on which 'camp' you belong to, within those two sections are lots of other sub-sections, it is just so messy! I'm sure we can all agree that there is a need to have God-fearing persons in positions of power and authority that can govern and make the best decisions for the nation.

However, that doesn't mean they all have to be conservative. It doesn't even mean that they all need to be Christian! There are highly educated, intelligent, experienced, God-fearing people who may be of a liberal persuasion that are able to do just as fine a job as anyone else. Someone doesn't have to be Christian to be God fearing.

As far as I'm concerned, even though it would be nice if the candidate was a Christian, that's not number one on my list in an election cycle. However, that is an area of fear that has gone undiagnosed in the Church for centuries. The fear is that if we have a president who is not a Christian then abortions will rise, the nation of Israel won't be supported, there will be no law and order, and the nation will go down the tubes.

Most evangelicals don't see this as a spirit of fear governing their thought lives; they see it as being responsible Christians doing what Jesus would do. A person's political views are somewhat of a reflection of their values, and who they are as a person - not totally, but somewhat. The tendency therefore is for some spiritual leadership to espouse the virtues of the Republican political party until it spills over to their congregations.

It should be that I'm unable to think of anyone who would want to attend church on a continual basis to hear about a political party and how it best lines up with scripture. Yet there are thousands of people, some of whom I know, who do it joyfully every election cycle! It should be that we attend church services to hear about Jesus, His finished works, the

Gospel of His Grace, how to apply His Word to our lives, and things of that nature; not about the Pastor's candidate of choice and how to vote! I have a friend who said that she doesn't pay any attention to people who don't discuss racism and police brutality when speaking to her about voting. I love it!

Most Christians follow the Bible admonition to pray for our leaders and those in authority. I've seen the call-to-action prayers and the hundreds of prayer groups that have suddenly sprung up in churches within the last four years with a focus on praying for our president. I don't recall similar messages and call to action prayers like this during President Obama's tenure though. It could be because the Church decided to take sides. It wasn't enough to be Christian; we had to be Republican Christians and President Obama was not a Republican. God help us!

When did Jesus ever command us to choose sides and lead whole congregations into choosing sides as well? The only side we're to be on, is God's side. Presuming that God leans towards Republicans or Democrats based on our interpretation of the Bible is hazardous at the very least. Leading congregations in that direction, is even worse.

When we marry ourselves to a particular allegiance, we've then lost the ability to see that we don't have all the answers. It's at that point that we believe that what we know, and the side we're on, and our camp, has all the answers. Our pride then takes the stage front and center. It was sad to see that as the Church picked political sides; what was right really wasn't as important anymore as winning and promoting 'our conservative side.' The issue now is that the opinions of the right and the left could both be wrong, as neither side has all the information needed.

I really believe that the way God intended for this to flow was for us all to work together, rather than choosing which side we felt aligned best with our interpretation of the Bible and then presented it to our congregations. Thus, there is the great divide.

FOCUS ON POLITICS

The continued evangelical focus on politics continues to taint Christianity as we know it. Since neither the Gospel, nor our faith can be contaminated, it really is possible to become a Christian by grace through faith and have it to be all about Jesus.

What a concept! There are many non-evangelical Christians who have not sold out their souls to continued division. There are Christians who love Jesus, love His Word and love people. Could it be that the body of Christ in America has lost its witness because we decided to take political sides? In my eyes, the answer is yes. This is part of what the conservative label has done. It has lumped us into a pile with everyone else. (The Liberal Christian label has also done the same thing). Instead of the body of Christ standing out, being the beacon of light, the city set on top of the hill, we're now given the side eye.

Some people hear you're a Christian and they immediately think you hate immigrants, the LGBTQ community and everyone working in an abortion clinic or who has had an abortion. We've told President Obama to go back to Africa, we've sided with those who have challenged his place of birth, and we've called his wife a gorilla in heels. I've even seen a post on my Facebook feed where someone that sang in the choir with me said that President Obama should be tarred and feathered. Yep!

What's even worse was other Christians that I know and have been in prayer groups and choir with for several years 'liked' the post! The only person to comment and call her out on her racist post; was me. She never removed the post and never responded.

That following Sunday she was back in the choir belting out those alto notes as only she could! A strange thing has happened since then though. Here we are years later, and the same person is back on Facebook quoting Romans 13:1-2 to anyone that will listen, telling us all to respect the office of the president and reminding us to pray for him. Where were her prayers for the last administration?

Where was her respect for the last president? I sometimes feel like we think the rest of the body of Christ as well as the world, aren't noticing what the Church has been doing and to a large extent still does! That's just one example of something that's personal, but I've seen this trend ever since I became born again. Each election cycle builds upon itself and here we are!

This is what the narrow label of conservatism has to offer. And it's not just the conservative label that the body of Christ has married. There are other labels that we've adopted. You may hear some churches described as a Pro Israel church, Christian right church, or Christian left church, and that's outside of the denominations!

Labels demand that sides be chosen. Labels demand that everyone stays with the chosen side, or you run the chance of being alienated from the conservative box.

VOTE THE PLATFORM

"We're not taking sides, we aren't voting for the party or the person, we're voting for the platform." Have you ever heard anything quite like that at your church? There are churches where this is taught, and it has

proven to be mentally destructive and divisive. Great damage has been done within the Church and great damage has been done to the Church with this teaching. Most of us just want the Gospel preached and the Gospel is the good news of Jesus Christ.

The Gospel is not the good news of how good your party will be for America, and how great America will become again. Many believers have now backed away from church and from their church friends, because they believe that the Gospel has become secularized and politicized and that things are irreversible. But nothing is irreversible when God is involved.

If you dare to come against the logic of vote-for-the-platform-not-the-person/party, you're going to find that there are many hoping to convince you that their way is the right way, and that if you don't vote that way, the United States of America will not be blessed by God.

"The next president is going to be very vital ... in freeing up your religion, freeing up your thoughts," Trump said. "You really don't have religious freedom."

In June 2016 in New York City, Candidate Donald Trump met with evangelical leaders. At that meeting he mentioned that ministers were petrified to talk about politics because of IRS rules and suggested that he was going to 'get rid of it'. He also told them that he would give them religious freedom because they didn't really have it. When he said that to the evangelicals present at the meeting that day, I believe that was when their grandiose ideas of what Donald Trump could do for the Church, if he was elected, settled into their hearts.

The excitement began: We could talk all the politics we wanted to from the pulpit, endorse our favorite candidate (God's choice), and we no longer had to be concerned about same sex lawsuits or the transgender community using the same bathrooms with our daughters. Our prayers were being answered at last! Imagine a president who could give us back our religious freedom! I'd like you to think about this for a minute though: If any president of these United States can do something for the Body of Christ that Jesus Christ the Messiah is unable to do, then surely you and I are serving the wrong god.

This is narrow conservatism once again to the rescue! We have faith in the Republican candidate, faith in the Republican president, faith in what the Republican president promised to do for the Church, and we even have faith in our own faith. The Bible says, *"Have faith in God."* (Mark 11:22). Faith that comes from the Word of God is the God-kind of faith that works when we put it to work. If the God-kind of faith that you have is only being used when you pray for Republicans then that's not an indictment against the Democrats, it's an indictment against you.

Couldn't we have used the same God- kind of faith to pray for a democratic president and administration when they were in office and expect answers to our prayers as well?

Much of what conservative evangelicals once believed about the moral status of their candidate of choice was shoved to the side in the 2016 and 2020 elections, because of their marriage to the Republican party. Congregations stared in wide-eyed disbelief as church leaders shamelessly courted the conservative label. 'Go ye into all the world,' suddenly turned into, 'Make America Great Again'.

Many evangelicals, trusting in the words of spiritual leaders rather than hearing from God for themselves, took the political path that was shown and kept on walking. Some are still walking, trying to figure out what on earth happened.

Ultimately it was a risk many were willing to take because they were hell bent on not voting for the person but the platform. If you're voting for the platform rather than the person or the party that means that anyone occupying the space of the Republican party platform will receive your vote.

Anyone. Even if that person was Hitler. Even if that person was someone who consistently attempted to bully people. Even if that someone continuously spoke ill of and demonized the same people groups that sit in your congregation every week to hear you preach to them about living according to the Word of God. Here is my opinion: Voting the platform is voting the person and voting the platform is voting the party.

GOD IS BACK IN THE WHITE HOUSE!

I've heard the *'God-is-back-in-the-White-House'* sermon, and the *'We've got our nation back',* sermon as I'm sure you may have as well. Depending on what your thoughts are about conservative evangelicals, those two phrases could be translated to mean: 'Yeah, our brand of Jesus and white supremacy are returning to the White House!'

Or it could mean: 'Thank you God, our prayers helped to get the nig*er out!' Or it could mean, 'We finally have a God-fearing president who will do right by Israel and make this nation great again!' I'm sure if you consider yourself to be a conservative evangelical and you believed that God was not in the White House during the Obama (or any democratic) administration, there are most likely many more sentences you can add to these.

In the meantime, some people listening to this narrative want to know: *When was America ever great? What period of time would you be referring to? What is the Church's part in making America great again?*

Then those in favor of making it great again may think: *What do I have to do to help this president and the Republican party to make this nation great again? What scriptures should I pray so that my Pastor and our church could do our part in making America great again?*

And if you consider yourself to be a conservative evangelical leader in the church, you are most certainly hearing from 'God' as He is telling you what scriptures you should preach about to make sure that America becomes great again. (I told you it was messy…)

This could be one reason why fewer and fewer want nothing to do with our brand of Christianity or evangelicalism. Scripture has been used to justify some of the greatest atrocities in human history. People were tortured and burned to death based on someone's understanding of the scriptures. Jesus Himself faced His greatest opposition from those who knew the scriptures!

Knowing the scriptures is one thing, rightly dividing it, is another. During the great rejoicing within the evangelical church after the 2016 elections, there was a false calm that settled into many pulpits as presidential prayer groups were springing up once more. Happy days are here again! Finally, we were getting what we prayed for after believing God for this to happen for eight long years, this is such a joy to behold!

God has answered, and we have a man who has God's heart, one who will take the country in the right direction. I don't think that we realized that just as our prayers were helping the President Trump, those same prayers could have done that for the last president before him, yet some churches, prayer leaders, and prayer groups decided to stop praying.

We shut down some of our presidential prayer groups because we didn't get a Republican win as God wanted.

Our narrow conservative ideology combined with undiagnosed cognitive dissonance didn't allow for our minds to dwell in that space. Who put God out of the White House? Is God Omni-Present depending on who is in the White House, or is He everywhere all at the same time as our Bibles declare?

I don't think we realize how that theology looks and sounds to people who are longing to get a taste of Jesus. The Church is in trouble, but our evangelical pride won't allow us to see it. Where was God for the eight years when President Obama was there? Did He leave the White House because the then-president was a Black man? Did He leave because the president was a Democrat? Did He leave because he was a Muslim? Perhaps He left because we, the narrow conservative church, dis-banded our prayer groups after the democratic president was put in office?

There are so many directions in which this could go. This is why the conservative label, or any label, is narrowing! It halts our perspective, narrows our vision, and interrupts heaven's flow of revelation knowledge and wisdom to us all!

Is this the only tea that we can find to serve to our church members and to the world? The world is hearing us and they're watching us. They're not drinking the tea they're standing on the sidelines watching the judgmental horror show. They're not coming into our churches by the thousands. A lot of the world's population; want nothing to do with us! Unfortunately, it's not just the world that feels that way, some of the Church do as well.

The Church made moral compromises for the sake of politics, and there is now a gnawing sense that the division in the body of Christ has become wider, as many of our spiritual leaders continue to remain mum about their support of racism, bigotry and homophobia as evidenced in their support for those who promote it. The political Church has taken the platform and now that the 2020 elections gave us a democrat for president, here we go again! Politics is still weighing heavier than evangelism to the lost, as we re-strategize for the 2022 and 2024 elections.

Church leadership sold itself out to the highest political bidder in order to get another Republican win and when it didn't happen in 2020, instead of getting on our faces in humility and repentance before God, we doubled down and are now unable (because of cognitive dissonance) to accept the election results... Messy. Within the Church, there is the (unseen to the physical eye) war over liberalism versus conservatism.

How and why the Church became embroiled in this bitter battle, when Jesus called us to be fishers of men, has escaped me. *'I'm Conservative. I'm Liberal. I'm strictly left wing.'* Why and how did this happen? Who asked us to choose sides? Why can't we just teach believers how to follow the Holy Ghost, instead of teaching which 'side' is better based on our fleshy biases? Why can't we trust God with our nation instead of attempting to manipulate our 'camp' with our brand of politics?

I'll tell you why. It's fear, and that did not come from God! Surely congregations everywhere can read their Bibles for themselves and when we read for ourselves, we'll find out that Jesus never told us to choose between liberalism and conservatism, but He did tell us that He would send His Spirit to be our Teacher and Guide, and that His Spirit would disclose things to us:

John 16:13-15
Amplified Bible, Classic Edition (AMPC)

[13] But when He, the Spirit of Truth (the Truth-giving Spirit) comes, He will guide you into all the Truth (the whole, full Truth). For He will not speak His own message [on His own authority]; but He will tell whatever He hears [from the Father; He will give the message that has been given to Him], and He will announce *and* declare to you the things that are to come [that will happen in the future].

[14] He will honor *and* glorify Me, because He will take of (receive, draw upon) what is Mine and will reveal (declare, disclose, transmit) it to you.

So, shouldn't church leadership teach congregations how to hear and follow the Holy Spirit? I know some reading this will say, *"I made up my own mind before/when I got to the voting booth, no one forced me."* I'm positive that this is true. However, have you taken into consideration the subtle religious sermons about which platform is better than which, what the 'other side' stands for, what 'our camp' believes, and that what 'they' stand for is not what Jesus would stand for?

Have you ever thought about the fact that the way you and I think right now is based on what we have heard over several years at church? I am right now in the process of unlearning some things that were taught to me in error. We haven't given much attention to the years of snide comments against liberals, leftists and all the other names that the 'other side' has been called by our 'camp.'

At the same time, those who belong to churches where the liberal agenda is pushed can attest to the fact that the same thing is done when referring to conservatives. This is not who Jesus Christ has called His body to be!

CONSERVATIVE FEAR-BASED POLITICS

We've discussed that the majority of Conservative Christians have always rooted for the Republican candidate, because of the belief that the Republican platform best lines up with what God wants for America. We've seen that we desperately wanted the Republican candidate to be that person that we had been praying for, for several years.

What we also saw was that our spiritual leaders kept ignoring the things that were said and done by the last administration that adversely affected the congregations gracing their pews on Sunday mornings. *'What do you mean by addressing the situation? There's nothing to address!'* In our minds, one has nothing to do with the other.

We wanted a Republican in office, we got one, and now we don't much care about who is affected because we know that God is pleased! We're now on a mission to turn the nation around in the right direction and nothing but narrow conservatism will do the job! What we believed was that President Trump would have placed the United States on a pathway of blessing and that things would have turned around for the nation after his election.

No more hurricanes, tornadoes, or earthquakes because the right person was in office. The churches that pray the 'right way' will not see any harm or danger come to their congregations. The way we've been trained to think is sadistic, and if Covid-19 didn't wake up the body of Christ, I don't know what will.

Narrow conservatism thinks that bad things will happen when a democrat becomes president. I'm not sure what story was being spun as an excuse for what happened during the last 4 years of the Republican administration. The last Republican president left, and the nation is in more turmoil now than it has ever been, but watch closely and you'll see that somehow you and I (the Church) will be blamed for this. If we, the ones sitting in the pews aren't blamed, then for sure it'll be because of the Obama administration, LOL! We're either; not praying right, not showing up often enough for church services, not giving enough, or all the above. This is fake faith, real fear and narrow conservatism acting out.

The idea that Christians are voting differently from each other is nothing strange, it's healthy. I believe that the plan of God was for both political parties to work together as one, to make a better nation. No one party has all the answers, if we could work across the aisles to make things better for Americans and the world, why not?

No one could convince me that God is a conservative God, or that He only likes and honors conservative candidates, or that He would always want only a conservative in the office of the president.

That is an extremely narrow way of thinking. It is that kind of thinking that essentially places God in the toy box that we built for Him with our narrow thinking. God is much bigger than conservatism and He is not ever going to be bound by it! Many churches see every election cycle as a major work that we need to do, and to a certain extent, it is. However, it's not always about us, it's about what Jesus has already done. If His works are finished, what then is our job? Two things: (1) Fear not. (2) Only believe.

Luke 8:50
King James Version (KJV)

50 But when Jesus heard it, he answered him, saying, Fear not: believe only, and she shall be made whole.

The 'fear not' is where I believe we stumbled. Every election season, you'll see religion, (that has always had a front row seat) and fear come right up to the pulpit, take another giant foothold in the Church, and attempt to crush and oppress us with more works of the flesh. We ignore the spirit of religion because we've become very familiar with it over decades, and we believe that it is God's Spirit.

We quickly begin to initiate prayer groups, giving them specific topics to pray over as it relates to blessing the candidate of our choice and rebuking (cursing) the other candidate. Our focus is on another 'savior' in the form of a Republican president. I don't believe that it ever occurred to us that God can supernaturally use both parties, both sides, regardless of who's in office. The spirits of fear and religion have led us to think and act this narrow-minded way and are also the driving forces behind the thought process that causes us to believe that if our Republican party isn't in office, or if our Republican candidate isn't holding the highest office in the land, then the gay community and Black and Brown immigrants will run (and ruin) our lives. Conservative evangelical leaders pastor a group of highly intelligent people who can decipher information all on their own. Additionally, we have the greatest Helper in the world to assist us in the decision-making process, the Holy Spirit.

What we're looking at is fear mongering. Fear that our congregations will not vote how we want them to, fear that the wrong party will be put in office, fear that we will all be judged by God for the error, fear that the curse (that was already done away with, in Jesus) will come to get us. Pastors, leaders, if you don't trust that the messages you've preached to your congregations over the years will enable them to make decisions as they are led by the Holy Spirit; then what's the use? What have they learned from listening to decades of your messages?

If we've been taught well (and I know that in the last couple of years, I have been), then all that's left to do now, is for our leaders to pray over both parties/candidates and allow the congregation to be led by the Holy Ghost. If someone goes to their church for pastoral counseling about voting, then maybe I could see the leader using comparisons of both parties; but yet again... the counseling given will most likely be 100% skewed with the way the leader thinks, rather than what the Holy Spirit is saying. For me, based on what I've endured over the years; the chances that both the leader and the Holy Spirit are saying the same thing during an election cycle are highly unlikely.

Fear... The thing that we most preach against is the thing that is our driving force, and we haven't realized it. You may have heard it from a pulpit near you, that it's a candidate's stand on abortion that will seal the deal and catch votes for conservatism. If not, then we're not playing with that candidate! That is another narrow way of thinking. Look, God can use anybody, at any time, to do any job He wants done. He has chosen to do it with us, His body, but He can do it without us.

A sure-fire way to know when God is not involved in something; is the amount of confusion and chaos left in the aisles after our crucial decisions have been made.

When we go home confused about what we heard at church, or we're bewildered by what we hear coming from the pulpit, from the same leaders who have preached against fear in previous years, then, we have a problem. When we no longer want to fellowship with people of like precious faith because we suddenly don't know what party or candidate they favor, we have another problem.

When relationships become strained because I believe that the Pastor heard God about the next president, but you believe that the Pastor was wrong about what he said he heard, then there's another problem.

1 Corinthians 14:33
King James Version (KJV)

33 For God is not the author of confusion, but of peace, as in all churches of the saints.

If we're anxious and worried about elections (or anything else, for that matter) as we pray, it's either because we don't believe that God is able, or we don't believe that He's willing. The reason we study the Word is to show ourselves approved onto God, not so that we can correct each other and show who is wrong and who is right, or which side is better than the other.

We've taken the Gospel and brought it down to its lowest common denominator, which is, ourselves. We've interpreted God's Word with our little minds instead of by His Spirit. What I heard from a large majority of evangelicals concerning the 2016 and 2020 elections was fear-based. Fear that if we ended up with a liberal Supreme Court, Christianity would be done away with (which is really idolatry, because we're idolizing the Supreme Court above our God).

We don't need the Supreme Court to save souls, that's our job and we have the Holy Spirit as our Advocate. The Supreme Court makes decisions based on the constitution. God makes His decisions based on His Word! There could be also in some cases, the fear of losing the 501c3 status, which enables churches and ministries to escape taxes for purchases, and to build homes without feeling the pinch of property taxes.

Then there is the Johnson Amendment. Some churches couldn't care less about this amendment that prohibits churches from endorsing or opposing political candidates. They're so busy preaching the Gospel of Grace, they don't have time to coerce their congregations into casting a Republican vote.

Then there are other churches that spend a lot of time praying and confessing for the Amendment to be overturned, so they can continue manipulating their congregations on political issues, albeit on a much larger scale. The manipulation and bullying must stop. Please don't bully your way through with scripture to make others see your point of view concerning their right to vote for whomever they're led to vote for. God gave us all the right to choose.

If we have anything to do with it, let us just present the facts and let people choose. Shaming or degrading them based on who they decide to vote for is unacceptable! Thankfully, nothing and no one can topple God from His throne. However, hypocrisy and the abuse of spiritual power can slowly but surely drive people away and temporarily destroy God's family unit.

I can almost guarantee you that the State you live in, and the city within that state, largely determine what you hear at church concerning politics. Most houses of worship don't care much who the candidates are because if there is the letter R attached to their name, we're all going to have to 'obey God' and vote for them.

No discussion needed or necessary. There had been division in the Church way before the last election cycle, but it became so much clearer after the 2016 and the 2020 election season. I believe that the division needed to be exposed and dealt with. We've seen it, now let's deal with it. There has been some measure of change, however. Politics responds greatly to pressure, so what I see that is of paramount importance, is that the election of President Donald Trump brought out and is continuing to bring out the toughest, smartest, most hardcore, and beast mode women that this country could possibly imagine, as evidenced in the November 2018 primaries where a record total of 125 women were elected to office.

It's interesting to me that some of the very things we try to talk our children out of doing and being, were okay during the last election cycle. We try to talk them out of disrespecting women, bullying others, name calling, lying, sexual assault, etc.

Some churches have had to fire their staff for sexual misconduct, but then at the same time, they ask their congregations to vote for someone just like the person they just fired, all in the name of the Republican elephant. Yes, I understand about forgiving and forgetting that is the thing to do. What bothered me was the hypocrisy. I've seen a side to my fellow Christians that I now cannot un-see, and it has shaken me to my core.

I always knew that something was wrong with this narrow way of life, but I couldn't quite put my finger on it until I was introduced to the term, 'The Narrowness of Conservatism'. I now see that some of the things I had been taught, and what I was led to believe as a result, caused me to mentally live in a narrow and divisive place! This narrow way of conservatism has done a lot of damage to the body of Christ and needs to be repaired. It's time for the

Church to have deep, honest conversations. Our determination to alienate those who don't think and believe the way we want them to, has caused the Church to be viewed as a personal clique. I've been to churches where you couldn't get into that clique if you died on the cross and came alive again.

The clique is where conservatives make power moves that aren't really based on right versus wrong, Godly versus ungodly; instead, they are made by ego, pride, and in many cases, white supremacy. While our conservative evangelical neighbors are unable to stand up for righteousness because they're kneeling in their closets praying, you and I are going to have to be the ones that take a stand for the marginalized, downtrodden and those who don't have enough.

It would be interesting to find out how many people have turned off Christianity because of our behavior. We lost our sense of direction, confused congregations and lost thousands of churchgoers in the process. But who cares? We are conservative champions for the cause of Christ! Now, some who previously hid their hideous beliefs have now been emboldened to step out of the shadows and manifest the hatred they've held back for decades.

They are unafraid to show their faces in broad daylight as they protest with tiki torches and confederate flags. The silence of the Church as this is going on is deafening! I've heard the term 'alt right Christianity' but I want no part of it. I don't believe we should be supporting what the alt right supports, yet at the same time claim to be followers of Jesus Who loved the vulnerable and the outcast.

Now the world sees our lies, half-truths, and double standards. We're attempting to force people to accept our viewpoint and obey our religious laws, then we act surprised when they retaliate and walk out of the church never to be seen again!

If you cruise through the different social media platforms, you'll come across the divisive political rhetoric from born again, Holy Ghost filled believers:

'Republicans are sheep, and Democrats are goats, Republicans are saved, and Democrats are not; the Bible predicted the unholy Democrats 2 thousand years ago, so we need to vote them out.' The ugliness between the body of Christ and the body of Christ, the war between evangelicals and evangelicals and the war between Christians and Christians is being viewed by the world.

THE SILENCE OF THE CHURCH

The silence of the Church at times like these bothers me. I don't know of any church that has addressed the issues head on from a biblical perspective, although I'm sure that there are some who have. I do know that we need more voices. I saw where one Pastor on social media did mention that he did not agree with some of what President Trump was saying (he didn't say what part of the hateful rhetoric he didn't agree with, so I don't know).

But he did say that he didn't agree with **some** of it. I'm not sure if there is a fear in houses of worship that the regular tithing members will stop tithing if certain issues are discussed from the pulpit; or if Pastors don't want the prominent white members to leave if they begin addressing issues that affect minorities.

Either way the silence isn't good. How do we stand shoulder to shoulder with the obvious hatred that is leveled against minorities, the LGBTQ community and the immigrant community and remain silent? Are the churchgoers saying anything to their leadership about their silence? Do you; or anyone else in the pews have access to someone on the leadership team who makes the decisions? Churchgoers are talking, oh yes, they are!

They may not be talking to their leadership, but they're talking to each other for sure! They know when something's wrong, and when to slip through the back doors of the church, and they're doing it. We got so caught up in elephants and donkeys and all the while what God really wanted was hearts that were after Him.

This is why it is so important to work on our relationship with Jesus. It's imperative that we know and understand when we're hearing His voice versus hearing the voice of a stranger. God wants His Body to demonstrate being led by the Holy Spirit. A Pastor doesn't need to try to sway the votes of his congregation so that his will, could be done, and his kingdom come, rather than God's will and God's Kingdom being taken care of!

I'm happy that there are still large groups of people who have given their hearts to Jesus, follow His teachings, take the Bible seriously, and attend a church regularly. They work diligently to help the poor, those with addictions, and fight for human rights.

I know some genuine Jesus-loving Christians, who believe God and His Word and love their fellow man. Some have realized that nothing has been said about the state of the nation and the minorities in their congregations and they're praying for change. There are Christians who haven't committed themselves to any political party, they vote as they're led by God's Spirit committing themselves to God and His Word. I know several of them. If you identify with this paragraph, I am truly thankful to God for you!

Chapter 5

RACISM IN THE CONSERVATIVE CHURCH

HIGHLIGHTING BLACK WOMEN:

SHEREESE FRANCIS was a 29-year-old woman who was killed in New York City after her family called the authorities seeking help. Shereese, who had been diagnosed with schizophrenia, wasn't taking her medication. When she tried to leave the room against their orders, she was allegedly tackled by the police officers.

The Medical Examiner ruled her death a homicide with the cause of death being 'compression of trunk during agitated violent behavior (schizophrenia) while prone on bed and attempted restraint by police officers.' Rest in peace and power, Shereese!

THE AFRICAN SOUL

I was sitting at a service at Times Square Church many years ago and Pastor Teresa Conlon said, *"There has always been a battle for the African soul."* (If I remember this correctly, I believe that she was talking about a trip she made to an African nation, I don't remember which one). That statement went right through me when she said it and stayed with me for a very long time. I knew she was right, and I also knew that if she didn't say it for anyone else that day, she said it for me!

Years later, when I began to pray over and write *'The Narrowness of Conservatism'*, that statement rose up again in my spirit, and I knew that I couldn't write a book about the evangelical stand for narrow conservatism without including the horrors of Black and African American lives within the body of Christ.

I am a Christian woman, and I am Black. Being in Christ supersedes my blackness, but it does not erase it. It was God Who decided what color I would be and the same for you. Yes, God sees color, He sees my color and He sees yours. I believe He wants us to see each other's colors too!

I've heard this more times than I care to remember, *"I don't see your color."* You just decided to dismiss the color of my skin because you feel like it? *"I see no color."* You know good and well that I'm Black. If you want to say something, anything about my color, how about instead of dismissing my color you say: *"I see your color and I value what you have to say. I will work hard against the racism that continually works against you. Please show me how to do better by you."* The daughter of Dr. Martin Luther King, Jr, the Reverend

Bernice King, said on Twitter recently, *"Racism is not dislike, bias or ill will toward another race. It is the power to obstruct justice, progress and equality."*

As racial divisions become more pronounced every day in the Church and in the world, the Church is yet to come to terms with how horrible its treatment of Black people has always been. There are issues with another man being different by having a different color skin, when all the while it was God Who created these differences in the first place!

We've not yet fully understood that we are to love one another and learn from each other's differences. Instead, one person believes they are more powerful than the other because of the color of their skin.

We've already established that the Democratic/ Republican rhetoric in the pulpit is totally unnecessary, but my reasons for mentioning it again here is because these efforts, as well as the blatant attempts to sway congregations to vote one way or another, combined with the participation of the Church in the horrors of systemic racism, are in my eyes the biggest failures of the American Church.

White supremacy and racism have been the BFF (best friends forever) of the Church for centuries and have gone undetected by most except for Black people who know first-hand what racism looks and smells like. For those non-Black people that do notice racism in the Church, they usually resort to prayer rather than using their voices to speak out.

There are several reasons for this: It could be that they are unaware that very little change for Black people will occur within the Church without the white voice, or it could be that since it doesn't affect them it's not really necessary to get involved by using their voices, they'd rather pray and let God handle it. Maybe they don't know what to do so they do nothing.

After a while even if acts of racism are observed, some have already become desensitized and have turned a blind eye. For Black souls however, we've become somewhat used to the daily micro-aggressions that come with living while Black in the Church and in the world. That is, until the recorded murder of George Floyd.

His murder stirred up a global movement that had most of the world coming together as one, on behalf of Black lives. At this moment in history many White people have joined the fight and that; combined with a global pandemic that caused a time of self-reflecting for many has turned what was once just a Black movement into a global cry for justice. Because the historical narrative of Black and African American people lacks truth it seems like reconciliation is nearly impossible but it's not. If we're the body of Christ that we claim to be, and we have God's spirit living in us, then we have the power to create change in those areas. We'll have to do the necessary work, and it's not just about hiding out and praying. It's about having open, honest, deep, raw, and uncomfortable discussions from the pulpit.

This isn't about your Pastor clenching his fist and shaking his hands towards the congregation saying: *"We are not tolerating racism in this church!"* While everyone including the front-row racists say, *"Amen!"* There's still much to be done outside of praise and worship, prayer, and the shaking of fists. David didn't kill Goliath in his prayer closet, and Nehemiah didn't build the wall in his closet either.

FORGIVING THE RACIST BULLIES

Most evangelical bullies use the label of conservatism to hide their racist views and agenda, but Black people are already hip to that as well as hidden sexism and other hateful ideologies, all in the name of the Lord.

That's why conservative teaching about voting for the *'platform not the person/party'* is riddled with religion and can also be another way of excusing racist behavior. What you're saying is: *"I don't care if this person I'm voting for hates Black people and Mexicans, and I don't care if their lifestyle emulates bigotry, I'm going to support them because this person is a Republican and I know that this is what God wants."* The churchy excuse for that is: If God chose the Apostle Paul who went around killing Christians, then he could choose my imperfect candidate of choice too! God did choose the Apostle Paul to carry out His mission in the earth.

The issue here is that the Apostle Paul was used by God to bring people together; not to cause division. Paul wasn't leveling racist comments at minorities every time he turned around.

What bothers me is that you're asking me to forgive racist comments and ideology and move on. Sure, I will forgive! Move on from racism? Absolutely not! How can we move on when it is still perpetuated in the Church, preached from the platform and is still responsible for the loss of millions of Black lives all over the world? Why is it that some church leaders are so comfortable promoting bigotry from their tax-free pulpits?

WHITE SUPREMACY AND WHITE SILENCE

Reverend Bernice King said in a tweet, *"Being respectful is about my standard for engaging others. Respectability is about me having to meet someone else's standards in order for them to respect me. And Blackness will never meet white supremacy's standards for being respected."* That is because white supremacy is heavy and pervasive. Black people are required to jump through racist hoops for the sake of avoiding being murdered in our own backyards! If you're White and you feel that it's because you always act the right way with the police, and you always comply with the requests of the police officers so that's why you're alive today, that's not true. You believe a lie. You're alive because of the color of your skin.

There are ranks of white supremacy in the police force and in the government. White supremacy is in our schools teaching our children; they're at the banks granting and/or declining loans to whomever they will. They sit on the boards of several top corporations, and they sit in the front rows at local churches. White supremacy is a huge money maker and a form of security for many White people.

It's the white silence from the pulpit that is so damaging. That white silence that continues to wound. It's the cover-up that could be frustrating to Black people if we let it. If as a leader in the church you expected something different, you thought things would have turned out differently after the 2016 election cycle when President Trump got in office, but it didn't, then it's OK to say that. Your congregation will have more respect for you if you do! It's when you gloss over racism and bigotry like they don't matter; that drives people away.

White supremacy and the alt right are incompatible with the gospel of Jesus Christ; the Church has no business sympathizing with it. The late great Archbishop Emeritus, Sir Desmond Tutu, South African Anti-Apartheid and Human Rights Activist said, *"If you are neutral in situations of injustice, you have chosen the side of the oppressor."* And Dr Martin Luther King Jr. said, *"In the end we will remember not the words of our enemies, but the silence of our friends."*

The white supremacists we see today weren't indoctrinated over-night; they've been around for decades. White silence is a form of terrorism because you see what's happening; you know it's wrong; yet you continue to make great gains off a system that was specifically designed to oppress Black people yet allows White people to live freely. You say and do nothing about it, because it does not affect you.

Oppression is being enforced by your silence! Most White people are aware that if they speak up something *may* change for the Black person, yet they choose not to. Jesus Christ spent a lot of time in prayer to receive wisdom from His Father; then He went out and put that wisdom into motion.

We will have to do the same. What do you think would happen if every White person that knows that the system of racism is wrong rose up and said something about it? Or joined in with a cause that was helping to eradicate it? Or used their voices or social media platforms to raise awareness and eradicate the system and the stigma associated with it? I'll tell you what will happen: There will be great fear throughout the nation because many White people (Christians included) are quite comfortable with their mentally and physically un-oppressed lives and have zero desire to step out of that comfort zone.

Therefore, those that do step out will face a lot of backlash, resistance and resentment which has the potential of leading to the fear of speaking out in the future. However, it will surely put a dent into the brick wall of systemic racism that's been hovering over the Church for decades and will continue to, unless we find a way to work together.

THE AWAKENING

There was a word of prophecy given to the body of Christ about an awakening back in 2008. We've been praying for that awakening unto God since 2008 and the awakening unto God is here! God has awakened us to the lies we've been told at church. He has awakened us to racism in the pulpit and He encourages us to speak out.

He has also awakened us to the importance of our personal relationship with Him rather than a personal relationship with our Pastors and spiritual leaders.

He has awakened us to white supremacy holding the purse strings in some churches. He has awakened us to the racism status quo and undercover racists holding key positions in churches and ministries, stifling diversity and growth. The awakening is taking place on the streets, as multiplied thousands are protesting racism and police brutality with fists held high!

If you can't see the awakening yet, ask the Lord to show you. You may be surprised as what He reveals. Those who want to stick their heads in the sand and wait for an awakening to look the way or happen the way that they think it should look or happen may be very disappointed.

If you're not in favor of speaking out against hatred and bigotry that has become commonplace in the Church and is likely to escalate - you may be a big part of the problem. I don't see anywhere in scripture where Jews were asked to operate outside of their Jewishness, or where the Gentiles were called on to give up their culture. Yet on many occasions, Black people are required to dress and style our hair in a way that is acceptable to the white gaze, in order for us to come anywhere near the pulpit of many churches, or for us to be hired for jobs.

Jesus stood up for the marginalized and those deemed outcasts by society. Do you believe that Jesus would have asked a Black person to undo their braids or cut their locs so that they could become a disciple and follow Him? Part of the problem that encourages this type of thinking is the spirit of religion. The spirit of religion and the spirit of racism are best buddies. When you find the spirit of racism, the spirit of religion won't be far behind.

LAW AND ORDER

People who benefit from white supremacy often call for law and order, and the call is loud and clear. Most evangelicals that are calling for law and order are White with absolutely nothing to lose in a white nationalist society. As Christians why would we want to uphold systems that cause oppression, thereby giving us power over someone else?

Doesn't our power come from God? To me, asking for law and order/civility is code for, '*Make the Black people shut up. Make them sit down*'. But Ha! Keep on dreaming honey, because we will never be silent. How could we? Why should we?

I am sure most won't understand because they've never lived it, so telling Black people how to feel about racism, what parts we should forget about racism, or who we should forgive and when, is highly inappropriate and totally out of order. Christians already know that forgiveness is a given.

Instead of calling for law and order, how about making the decision that it's high time for White Christians to let their White spiritual leaders know that they're disappointed that they've not addressed matters affecting their Black brothers and sisters? The integrity of the Church is at stake, your relationship with your brothers and sisters of color is at stake and so is your relationship with Jesus.

The atrocities, hate language, Nazi sympathizers etc., have been marinating for centuries in the Church, and it is now overflowing. Oh wait… we did pray for *'the overflow,'* now, didn't we? Whoa! It looks like prayers are being answered, and not in the manner that we thought they would. Yikes! I thank God that the Gospel of Grace is the good news of Jesus' Grace, so that His Grace can help us to overcome our human inhibitions in this multi-cultural community called the Church.

If you believe that raising the issue of race is un-Christian or that talking about racism at church causes confusion or frustration, your argument is riddled with ignorance. We all have things to learn about each other and unity starts with each one of us individually.

RACISM, RACISM, PLEASE GO AWAY!

The hate language being spewed out of the 2016 election cycle spoke to some 'good Christian' folk in much the same manner as it spoke to the 'good Christian' slave owners in the past. This is a nation (and a Church) that is still struggling with the after-effects of the iniquity of slavery. If conservatives are continuously comfortable at practicing bigotry and the right to discriminate according to their religious beliefs, racism will never be addressed.

The First Amendment and the Constitution allows everyone to freely live according to their own beliefs. We cannot force others to conform to our beliefs and we cannot treat others badly if they don't believe the same way that we do. If we're using conservative Christianity as an excuse to promote contempt and judgment rather than acceptance and love, then we aren't being very Christ-like.

If we are claiming to be persecuted as we're seeking the legal right to persecute others, then we are being blind to our own evil. Praying that the will of the Lord be done is the right thing to do. However, it is not the only thing to do, as prayer alone is not going to make racism magically go away.

The truth is that the scriptures eventually will get into our hearts and come out of our mouths in faith and make things happen. In the meantime (since that doesn't happen overnight) as we operate in the vein of throwing scriptures at situations that we don't want to deal with, racism is continuing to operate unchallenged in many churches.

The unwavering support of large portions of the body of Christ for bigotry, racism and intolerance stands starkly against the values that we claim to hold dear and comes across to me as a defiant act of hypocrisy. The world is watching! **Racism isn't going away because we think it should. It isn't leaving because we tell it to go either.** There is a part that the Church must play!

Are we cognitively activated conservatives? Are we conservatives who are hearing and following the Spirit of God? If love is king and love is action, then show us the love! The days where you claim to love Black people who have been repeatedly harmed by the same system that has benefited you for generations, is long over.

9 MINUTES AND 29 SECONDS

Close your eyes and picture this: Your head slammed against hard asphalt with a knee on your throat, as the life slowly ebbs from your body. What do you think your thoughts would be during those final moments of your life? I don't know. I couldn't even bring myself to go there in my mind. If you're reading this and you are White, chances are you'll never in your life have to experience anything even remotely close to what I just described.

If you're Black, the chances of it happening to you are alarmingly high. The name *George Floyd* conjures up many memories and images of racism and bigotry that I've experienced, both inside and outside of the Church. I couldn't bring myself to watch yet another video of another Black man being killed on camera. The knee on his neck, choking the life out of him as he called for his deceased mom, lasted for 9 minutes and 29 seconds, as I'm sure you already know.

It brought me to tears, but I didn't sit around wondering why there were no arrests right away, because I know the drill. Black people have been crying out for justice for centuries without help in sight and with zero help from our local churches. It took the murder of yet another Black man to bring the world together this time. Why was this time different? It's really a combination of things: It was not just because George Floyd's murder had been recorded for the whole world to see, but also because all of America was on lock down due to the Coronavirus, and most were glued to their televisions.

There were many who were suffering job losses as well as the death of loved ones due to the virus; so there was almost a collective sigh and reckoning, as well as a national 'searching of the heart' as to what the future would or should look like. There were also a lot of White people that for some reason joined our outrage this time around, plus I really believe that this is an appointed time for racism in the Church to be judged.

There should be no more running, hiding, slipping, or jiving around discussions having to do with racism in our churches. To anyone who is church or ministry staff, when you see racism rearing its ugly head on your job, or in the church, it is your responsibility before God to speak up! God has opened a wide door of opportunity in the church for us to deal with racism and white supremacy, and it's up to all of us to make it work!

Yes, we need laws passed to protect the lives of Black people, and yes protests are in order, but we cannot go back to church as usual because if we do, it will only lead to more trauma in the Church. In this one instance you can consider me as a conservative too, as I'm trying to conserve Black bodies and Black lives! It's too late to turn back, we've already seen racism at its finest, OK Church, what do we do now?

The outrage (in some cases maybe fake) that George Floyd's murder caused set the Church directly under the spotlight. White Pastors, along with church and ministry leaders and officials who for decades never thought to mention a single word about racists and racism in their churches and ministries were suddenly scrambling to record videos about how outraged they were by *"George Floyd's death"* (maybe afraid to use the word murder?), and quickly brushed over how it happened as they let us know how sorry they were and that they were praying for Black people.

We appreciate the prayers, but it is my belief that many of the church leadership didn't plan on saying anything about the murder of George Floyd (most never do), but the outcry of the social media masses changed things for them. I thank God that some Pastors immediately thought of speaking to their congregations to instill hope and comfort, a message to let them know that the leadership will always be there for them.

Other Pastors just went about their business as usual, while some attempted to smooth things in the usual white way by judging Black people, telling us to calm down and reminding us that all lives matter… Ugh. We stand side by side at church, Black people and White as we worship the Lord together, but as a White person, when the church service is over you could leave church, get in your car, and drive home safely. The chances of that same scenario happening to a Black person aren't the same as yours. Am I saying that all Black people drive around afraid for our lives? No. What I am saying is that a large portion of Black people do! You can talk all you want about Psalm 91 and the protective power of the Blood of Jesus (I know that they work), but we all know that it is only the Church that is aware of the privileges we have in Christ.

People who don't know Jesus and don't have a relationship with Him and His Word have no idea what we're talking about when we 'plead the Blood,' (which isn't mentioned in scripture anyway, but that's another sermon.) Pleading the Blood of Jesus over racism isn't going to make it go away.

A SOCIAL MEDIA POST

I saw this post on Facebook recently: *"So do White lives matter? ALL colors matter! Why are Blacks a more important color? Thank God when we get to heaven it doesn't matter what color you are."*

Let me answer this question: The mere fact that we even need to tell others that our lives matter is already a huge problem. We say it because we are highlighting issues that only happen to Black people! Injustice, economic disparities, racial inequality, and the disparity of lives lost do not affect other communities like they do Black communities! If you say that you didn't know that I'd say that were lying.

What race is predominantly killed by police officers over-reacting? What race is followed when they walk through certain stores? What race of people get pulled over and have their vehicles searched on any given day? I heard a Preacher say (concerning the murder of George Floyd), that he didn't know why someone didn't jump in and move the officer's knee off George Floyd's neck.

That's ignorance and white privilege at its peak. Reverend, if you don't know why out of all the Black people standing there, no one tried to remove the officer's knee off George Floyd's neck, then you don't deserve to have Black people in your congregation. You just don't! The reason why no one did is because they knew that they would have been shot and killed too! How could this Pastor not understand that?

If these racists are kneeling on necks in broad daylight with video cameras on and people standing around watching, can you just imagine what they're doing behind doors in schools, churches, medical facilities, HR Departments, banks, and prisons?

Just today I saw where two members of the National Guard were removed from protecting President Joe Biden because of what they posted on their social media profiles. Be wary of anyone who says they're following Jesus Christ but continually participates in dehumanizing and devaluing the lives of others. I love the truth of God's Word as Jesus prayed that we would be one just as He and His Father were one.

John 17:20-23
New Living Translation (NLT)

[20] "I am praying not only for these disciples but also for all who will ever believe in me through their message. [21] I pray that they will all be one, just as you and I are one—as you are in me, Father, and I am in you. And may they be in us so that the world will believe you sent me.

[22] "I have given them the glory you gave me, so they may be one as we are one. [23] I am in them, and you are in me. May they experience such perfect unity that the world will know that you sent me and that you love them as much as you love me.

The oneness that Jesus prayed for will come to pass! It hasn't happened yet though. Just praying the scripture alone doesn't mean that it will happen overnight or that it will happen at all, if we don't add some works to our faith! Church, we're missing the works part of this. I understand that not everyone will be into the works part of making sure that our churches are racism-free because many in leadership are good friends with white supremacists who keep their churches financially afloat. In that scenario it could be difficult for a leader to rock that boat, so I'm not going to expect it from every leader, but I should be able to!

RACIAL DIVISION IN THE PEWS

The time for painting over racial issues with the paintbrush of three scriptures and group prayer is long over. If more churches taught on the Gospel of Grace, sin and hatred would have less dominion in the pews. If someone has a different opinion that doesn't mean that they are wrong - they just don't see things the way you do!

Your opinion is your opinion, it isn't the truth. Sometimes, you agree to disagree and walk away or shake hands... Except when it comes to racism. Racism is not an 'agree-to-disagree' issue. Racist-driven prayers spew out of pulpits on a regular basis, but sometimes it's unnoticeable because it's covered in faith and contains scripture.

All over the world Black people are treated differently than White people, and White people know it. In schools, in the criminal justice system, in housing, and yes, at church too. The chances of you being called in for a job interview anywhere with a Black sounding name are slim. Guess what? It can also happen when you're auditioning for the Praise team too! As much as most churches like the 'Black sound' on their praise teams and choirs, that doesn't always mean that you'll make it on the team. Sometimes your resume goes through the hands of the white supremacist Music Director and that will be the end of your singing ministry at that church, unless someone else with the heart of God takes over the music ministry.

To prevent that from happening; should we give Black children white-sounding names? I know someone that did that because they didn't want their children to have problems later in life. Let's face it: The body of Christ has now become the most racially divided group in this nation. American Christians of color that aren't of any particular political persuasion, watch in horror and disbelief as the support from among White American conservatives for the racist narrative in the nation and in the Church continues to swell without a peep coming from the pulpit.

I still find it challenging to realize that I have friends and acquaintances that chose to ignore all the above because of the Republican R next to the name as they cast their votes. Some have decided that I should be un-friended/un-followed on social media because I was posting "stuff that caused division". Others have let me know that as they've been in prayer "the Lord" has asked them to share a couple of scriptures with me, to show me that things will get worse for Black people before they get better and that better comes when we (Black people) get to heaven.

Many of them have sent articles for me to read and suggested books that would help me, all because I began to stand up for Black lives! One woman even went so far as to say that I shouldn't expect or ask for Justice but should *"silently trust God in my prayer closet"*. The nerve of these racist evangelical *'friends!'* It infuriates me but yes, I've blocked them all on social media.

Sometimes it appears that some of our churches are in favor of having a Black face in the room or a couple of Black faces on the church platform. Unfortunately, we can't just put one or two Black faces on our leadership team and think that we have just uprooted racism or racist actions in our churches. Some have been privileged to be in the room with their Pastors.

They're allowed to stand on the platform, hold a mic and sing or encourage the people yet still aren't allowed to sit at the table during negotiations, still unable to assist in making decisions that would affect the congregation (knowing that there are Black people in the congregation). This is how corporate America operates; to see the Church operating the same way is disheartening.

BLACK LIVES MATTER AND THE KU KLUX KLAN

Have we really come to the place where we are comparing those who are wrapped in Confederate flags and Nazi emblems to those who are fighting to prevent their lives from being taken by protesting police brutality? We're asking for Black people to not be murdered by the police! Why is that controversial in the first place? It takes more than just resisting the ideology.

We also need to reject their ideology outright without qualifications and caveats, and take a firm stand to protect anyone anywhere who is under attack; especially the Black lives because they are the most oppressed.

Comparing the Ku Klux Klan to Black Lives Matter is like comparing Jesus to Satan. The KKK lynched, dismembered, beat, drowned, murdered and debilitated Black people. They terrorized Black people, destroyed their towns, bombed their churches as they were supported by law enforcement! Pastor, can you not see the difference here? Before you compare and preach it from your pulpit, please show me where Black Lives Matter ever did the equivalent!

It could be mind-boggling when you realize that back then, most churches just outright refused to support their Black members, but since the Church has been rooted and grounded in racism, it's easy to see why this has been the case for so long. The reason some churches took a (maybe temporary) stand against the caught-on-camera murder of George Floyd is because they realized that other churches took a stand, and they didn't want to be bombarded by social media haters on their church and ministry social media pages. Speaking out against racism should have happened a long time ago!

Saying 'Black Lives Matter' is an assertion that Black lives have as much value as other lives. It does not mean that other lives don't matter. Other lives don't even have to say that they matter because they know that they do! How can someone not understand this? Black people know that their lives don't matter to most, even in the church. It's sad that this needs to be said but because of America's racist history along with our justice system, it must be stated. We should at least be able to agree that to compare Black Lives Matter to the KKK is wrong, but many White Pastors and church leadership don't know that.

White supremacy believes that White people are superior to people of other races and the extermination of people of color is high on their agenda. Comparing these two groups (Black Lives Matter and the KKK) and setting them on equal footing is preposterous. One side is calling for the annihilation of an entire race, while the other side is trying to stay alive and be treated equally. One group wants equal rights and the violence against them to stop, the other group wants to eradicate everyone else who doesn't look like they do. I'm not sure why we can't tell the difference. There is no comparison, Church! Please see if you can look at the words 'Black Lives Matter' with understanding and empathy rather than judgment.

Close your eyes with me again and picture in your mind your White son, brother or husband tied to a tree and whipped to death, or hung from a tree to die, or tied to the back of a pick-up truck and dragged to his death, or forced to lay on asphalt with a knee squeezing the breath out of him as he tries to call out your name then slowly dies.

Now tell me how you feel. I don't want you to think of it happening to a Black person, think of it happening to a White family member... *Your* son, *your* husband, *your* brother. If you're honest with me and you felt fearful, intimidated, disgusted, sad, or maybe you even cried, I want you to know that for hundreds of years, Black people have experienced those same emotions in one form or another every single day. Picture that. Every day!

Even though supporters of any group can take things too far to one side and eventually lose sight of their original purpose, that doesn't mean they are a hate group, and that doesn't mean that their causes should be invalidated. If you have the faith of God in you, then that faith demands that you pay attention to what's happening in your church and community.

Many White churches endorsed hatred during the civil rights movement and some clergy condemned the marches for equality, while others refused to discuss what was going on outside the doors of the church even though it affected many of their members. That same thing is still going on today.

Once upon a time at a church I was a member of, my Pastor mentioned to our congregation, that if we wanted to get news from a trusted source about what was happening politically in the nation, there was a TV show called *'The O'Reilly Report',* that we should watch to get accurate information. I watched the show once, based on the recommendation of my Pastor and quickly turned it off.

It made me want to vomit because I could hardly believe that my then-Pastor believed the bigoted rhetoric that was being spewed on that show enough to recommend it to the entire congregation! I thought: How could he recommend this racist TV show? Does he not hear what this man is saying? *Is my Pastor racist too?* Addressing systemic racism isn't negative, neither is it divisive. It is uncomfortable though, but still must be addressed especially in the Church!

We can dialogue about economic policies we can disagree on what song to sing and how to run the prison ministry. However, concerning racism... this must be addressed publicly, honestly, and with everyone, not just the Pastor's token Black friends who probably won't say much to him about racism anyway because they've been included in the Pastor's clique.

THE FACE OF RACISM IN THE CHURCH IS THE FACE OF SATAN IN THE CHURCH

There were many White Americans and evangelicals who hated Dr. Martin Luther King Jr. They perceived him as a troublemaker and were happy about his assassination, yet it seems like we've moved from hating him to loving him (only after he was killed), and that's not because racism is becoming less prominent in the Church, it's because we have mentally scrubbed and sanitized his history to make it easier for us to swallow.

His daughter, Rev. Bernice King said: *"Unjust racist systems aren't broken. They were built to dehumanize and disenfranchise Black people. We have to begin with that truth and with the beloved community as our ultimate goal, re-imagine the major sectors of society, from education to law enforcement."* She's right! Then there's this statement that has been attributed to the comedian Chris Rock: *"Notice that there is more pressure on Black people to stop talking about race, than there is for racists to stop being racist. The system doesn't want racism to end; it just wants us to stop talking about it."* He's right too! We're not going to stop talking about it though. We see from the above statements that the narrative of how broken the system is, is false. The system of racism works just exactly as it was designed to work! When we open our mouths to challenge the system, we're called names.

Whenever you hear someone referred to as the 'angry Black woman;' you should know that the person doing the name-calling is most likely another white supremacist bully trying to shut us up, or a Black person who is accustomed to performing for the white gaze - but that's not going to happen, we're not going to be silent about racism.

After the Charlottesville protests, Pastor John Carter said on Facebook (on August 16, 2017): *"The face of racism, prejudice and oppression is the face of Satan. When Satan shows his face, the only righteous side is the one that opposes him."* If we are the righteousness of God in Christ, then our side is the righteous side and that's the side that should be opposing Satan, rather than helping Satan, right?

So, let's have conversations about racism! To promote change people are going to have to be uncomfortable for a minute. It was uncomfortable for me to hear one of my White acquaintances say to me: *"I'm not a racist but I believe that he is racist* (referring to President Trump) *but I voted for him again because my 401K is doing great."* What did I do when I heard that? I tried hard not to puke and got off the phone.

A couple of days later after the 'I-still-wanna-puke-when-I-think-about-you' feeling went away, I had a discussion with her about what she said. Unfortunately, she didn't see anything wrong with what she said.

There are millions like her in the Church. She's forgiven, but I don't miss her. President Trump isn't the originator of racism, but his election sure did normalize things for racists, white supremacists, and those in favor of segregation.

America can't be great if in the rank and file of the body of Christ white supremacy continues to run some churches; Sunday sermons as well as Ladies Bible studies cater only to White members; and racist rhetoric and cliques are the order of the day.

Racism in the Church and the heights from which it operates can best be described as *'wickedness in high places'*. Racism is still running arm and arm with white supremacy within the Body of Christ.

Ephesians 6:12
King James Version (KJV)

[12] For we wrestle not against flesh and blood, but against principalities, against powers, against the rulers of the darkness of this world, against spiritual wickedness in high places.

BLACK RACISTS

If you're not disgusted with what you've read so far and you're still reading, let's go a little further. If you're already disgusted it's okay, I told you that this would be an uncomfortable conversation for Christians to have. Go drink some water, watch Netflix and come back tomorrow. I'll be right here waiting on you!

You may have had or heard conversations about reverse racism, so I want to clear that up. There is no such thing as reverse racism, it isn't real. There is prejudice, and there is systemic racism. Black people cannot be racist because there is no system set up by Black people to debilitate and oppress White people. *White people cannot be negatively affected by a system created by them for their own benefit and privilege.*

The system of racism aims to debilitate and oppress Black people and was put in place to obstruct justice, obstruct equality and obstruct progress among other things. There is currently in 2022 no such system set in place by Black people to hinder and obstruct White people, who are the dominant group here. Therefore, we cannot be racist against them. There is no such thing as Black racists because Black people do not control the money, the systems, or the power needed to damage the interests of White people. Black people are unable to oppress White people in the same manner with which Black people are oppressed.

Any allegation of reverse racism is in itself yet another form of systemic racism because when White people lie about reverse racism leveled against them, this has the potential to cause more unjust laws to be passed that will continue to further prevent Black people from getting ahead and can even get Black people imprisoned or killed! There will be more biased legislation, political grandstanding, and a host of other underlying factors that can damage any wealth that Black people may have gained, financial or otherwise.

As we were in the early stages of this nation and ever since, White people of wealth and stature have been influencing laws in such a way that their own power and financial benefits could continue to flow. Not much has changed, this is part of the way systemic and structural racism was set up.

There have always been unjust laws made to protect white wealth, so allegations of reverse racism if it struck a nerve long enough would also cause more gentrification, and the government sponsored displacement, or the housing discrimination etc. New legislation that would expand access to prosperity for Black families would continue to be a dream.

What looks like reverse racism could simply be a manifestation of continued resentment and exasperation with white privilege... If you are White, you may have experienced more than a fair share of prejudice from some Black people; much of which could have begun with a series of micro aggressions that we endure daily to the point where many of us tune them out, but we're extremely tired of.

Things like wanting to touch our hair, telling us that you prefer to see us wear brighter color clothing (which makes us then become more acceptable to you, because wearing brighter colors has the effect of brightening our skin), or letting us know how many Black friends you have.

Personally, I don't care about how many Black friends you have or who your Black roommate was in college. I love you, and I carefully ignore the micro-aggressions because in some cases, you're not even aware of what you're doing. People sometimes project onto others, what they grew up hearing in their households that they deem to be acceptable, but much of it is not acceptable, it's racist. When in the history of this nation did Black people ever have the power to negatively affect the lives of White people for 400+ years? Black people can be prejudiced, and we often are. On one of my social media posts about the injustice often served to Black lives, one of my acquaintances tried to convey that racism operated on both sides by commenting that there were some of her Black neighbors who were racist and weren't nice to her.

If they weren't nice to you, that, my sister, is not racism. Maybe those people were prejudiced, or maybe they just don't like you, but that is not what racism is. Your Black neighbors and their ancestors have zero power to negatively affect your life. They don't have the power, the authority, or the resources to oppress, debilitate, and hold you back!

They don't have access to such a system that could do that to you. They are not racists; they just don't like you! That happens sometimes. White privilege does not mean that your life isn't difficult. Neither does it mean that your life cannot be difficult, was never difficult, or will never be difficult.

White privilege means that the *color of your skin* will never *ever* be a determining factor in what is causing your difficulties. White privilege sees situations, things, and people through the lens of privilege. White privilege says: *"It's horrible that George Floyd was killed but rioting and destroying property really has to stop!"* Think about that sentence for a minute, and instead try saying: *"It's horrible that there is rioting, and property being destroyed, but the killing of Black men absolutely has to stop!"* Do you see the difference here? Please tell me you do!

I saw this on social media once and it stayed with me. As of the time of writing this book I couldn't find out who originally said it. The saying is: *"When you're accustomed to privilege, equality feels like oppression."* It's not really oppression, it's just your flesh acting out at the thought of losing some of your privilege.

THE BLACK PRESIDENT

I discovered that many White evangelicals lived by a different agenda when the racial tensions exploded in the Church after Barack Obama became president. The spirit of racism that has always been in the Church started to bubble up to the surface.

I have some conservative Christian acquaintances that I sat and worshipped with, whose Facebook pages are still to this day filled with President Obama in monkey face, and some *'Nigerian born, Muslim terrorist'*, posts about him. I've had a Prayer-Minister as well as a Pastor tell me that I should stay out of the sun because I was too Black. I'm quite happy that social media has brought a lot of racist evangelical leaders up front and center on our smartphones and the world is able to see what Black people have been (in some cases) quietly enduring at the local church. Racism is terrorism. Racists are terrorists. White supremacy is terrorism. White supremacists are terrorists.

BLACK ON BLACK CRIME

Where did the term 'Black-on-Black crime' originate? This book isn't about that topic, but I can tell you that Black people commit crimes against other Black people for different reasons.

It really should be called neighborhood crime because it often occurs among people living in the same neighborhood. The same thing happens with White-on-White crime, this isn't a social construct that is peculiar to just Black people. For some reason, some of the media deliberately focus on Black-on-Black crime to the exclusion of other demographics.

I read a 2015 article where The Department of Justice - Bureau of Justice Statistics (BJS) found that most violent crimes are committed by people who are the same race as their victims. The rate of white-on-white violent crime, it found, is about four times the rate of black-on-white crime. It would take just one second to realize that white supremacists frequently like to manipulate the crime statistics to claim that non-white minorities, particularly Black people are the source of most violent crimes against whites but that is not the case.

The BJS study demonstrated that some 57 percent of crimes involving white victims were committed by white perpetrators while only 15% were committed by Black people and 11% by Hispanics. It was similar for Black crime victims with 63% of the crimes committed by Black perpetrators, 11% committed by whites, and 6.6% by Hispanics. The overall report was *that "the percentage of intra-racial [that is, same-race] victimization was higher than the percentage of interracial victimization for all types of violent crime except robbery."* Also, I learned that "the rate of white-on-white crime (12.0 per 1,000) was about 4 times higher than black-on-white violent crime (3.1 per 1,000)."

Some of the reasons for neighborhood crime among Black people, could be racism induced poverty, or simply because it's a crime that the police will often let them get away with. If you don't believe me, answer this question: DaQuan robs Jamal, but DaQuan also robs Bob. Both crimes are reported. Guess which one of those two crimes DaQuan will go to jail for? You're correct! He goes to jail for robbing Bob! That's how systemic racism works. Even Black victims of violence sometimes don't even report it many times because they know (and maybe have already experienced) that justice for a Black person is different than justice for a White person.

What would it look like for DaQuan if these racist systems and restrictions weren't in place? Well, if there was no systemic racism, DaQuan wouldn't be in jail, because he wouldn't have robbed Bob. He most likely would have had his own money because he would have been hired at a job despite his locs and his beautiful Black skin.

He wouldn't have lost the roof over his head because he wouldn't have gone to jail. His job would have been easier for him to find without the stigma of a prison record, and he would even be able to vote! Can you see how systemic racism reinforces a plague on the Black community?

FREED FROM POVERTY

If you have been redeemed, then you are free from the curse of poverty. That's important to know because in the United States poverty is criminalized, it is used as a means of punishment. If you've been arrested and you or your family, do not have the money for bail there's a chance that you could remain incarcerated for years without a trial. This happened to Kalief Browder, who was sent to Rikers Island when he was sixteen years old, accused of stealing a backpack. He never stood trial and never was found guilty of any crime yet held at Rikers Island for three years! Two out of those three years he spent in solitary confinement. He refused offers for plea deals because he knew that he was innocent! Eventually, the prosecutors dropped the charges, and he was released. After his release he eventually killed himself at his mother's home in New York.

If you read the above account and your first thought was: *"Well, why did he steal the back-pack?"* ... then I can almost guarantee that you, are a very narrow minded conservative. To some evangelicals, morals only matter when they're convenient.

WHOSE FIGHT IS THIS?

If you are a Christian, racism is not 'their fight,' as in the fight of Black people. As the Church/the body of Christ, this now becomes 'our fight' because we are all a part of the family of God. Many churches often take a bold stand for Israel, but when it pertains to the Black community, all we get from church leadership are scriptures and a prayer?

If White people were hurting, then the whole Church would be hurting, but when Black people are hurting? Crickets. As Christians, we don't get to stand on the side, point fingers and rebuke racism. We use the voices we have; we use our platforms.

The demonic spirit of racism emboldens and empowers those who love it and enables them to quickly become the worst versions of themselves. This version displays itself in the Church for us all to see. Looking down the hallways of history we will see that the deep racial tensions that resurfaced at the 2016 elections revealed an extremely narrow, shallow level of evangelical conservatism. This is not the Church that Jesus Christ is coming back to receive.

MEDIA VERSUS BLACK PEOPLE

If you think that Black people are making a big deal out of nothing, pay attention to the narrative in the media that Black people are already hip to. Church leaders, prayer leaders and intercessors need to be aware of how the system works because quite often the mind is conditioned by what you hear about Black people in the news, and it can directly affect the way you pray for Black people, because it affects the way you believe.

If someone kills Jews in a synagogue, we hear: *"This is a hate crime!"* If someone kills Black people at a Church, we hear: *"Well, we're not yet sure of his intent."* Or, when there's been yet another shooting that has made the news, would you like to know how we know that the person committing the shooting spree is White? Because you'll hear the TV anchor say: *"The suspect is in custody."* If the suspect is not White, they are hardly ever *'in custody'*.

Instead, what you'll often see is a picture of a white sheet over the dead body on the sidewalk. That's how we know the suspect was not White. Don't you dare shoot up a church as a Black person because you're not going to get a hamburger (insert sarcasm emoji) after your shooting spree as Dylan Roof did, because most likely you'll be dead.

When white supremacist mass murderer Dylan Roof a twenty-one-year-old White male killed nine people at a church in Charleston, he wasn't shot at or killed. Instead, he was hungry, so the police officers got him a hamburger. A Black man that just killed nine people and by some miracle just happened to still be alive to make it to the police station, would die from starvation first before anything like that happened. You know it and I know it.

When a crime has been committed and the suspect is Black, the media instantly lets us know that, as they furiously try to find out if the suspect has a police record. If the suspect is White however, the media finds the person's high school graduation picture or a family photo and that's the picture everyone sees on TV. If the suspect is Black, you'll get a picture of their mug shot if they have one, or a picture in a hoodie or some other outfit that stereotypes the Black person as a sinister-looking menace to society. Everyone knows that crack cocaine has been flooding the Black community for decades without there being any help for the addicts. Instead, they were highly criticized and incarcerated, and many are continuing to be imprisoned daily.

However, now that the addiction has hit the White community, suddenly the addicts are 'victims' in need of help, and there are Opioid Abuse and Addiction training classes. Can anyone spot the inconsistencies here? These are things Black people are accustomed to, but as we continue to use our voices to create change, we and our communities will be helped. It would be awesome if we could have the help of the local church in the fight to rid our communities of this evil.

In much the same way as different strokes for different folks, the labels placed on Black people are very different to those placed on White people, for the same action: If White people cannot find a job it's because of a bad economy. If Black people cannot find a job, it's because they're lazy and they want public assistance/welfare. It's interesting that Black people were only thought of as lazy after we stopped working for free on white owned plantations!

Back in the day everyone had Black people picking their cotton and cleaning their houses and nursing their babies. Since that stopped, suddenly we're lazy! If White people have a position of influence on the job, it's because of their hard work, but a Black person in the same situation, it can only be the result of affirmative action. These racist conversations don't just take place in the world they occur at church as well.

If you're in a predominately White Church, are you seeing the faces of Black and Brown people in the church media advertising your church activities, or on church flyers? Summer camp for the kids, or church picnics and Ladies Bible Study advertisements have all mostly featured our White counterparts. The world is now learning about this, and they have been including more people of color in their advertising.

The Body of Christ must catch up. Diversity is important and it helps our children, especially those of color, to see their future selves in different positions in life. The role the media plays is huge, whether you and your family pay attention to the TV, radio, movies, or not.

Cultural imperialism occurs when one nation's media is dominant in many other nations and even becomes the prime form of entertainment. The United States, (which still exports images of a White Savior (Jesus) but also displays people of color as being savage on a regular basis), has the worldwide monopoly in the media industry right now. The trickle-down effect that often comes neatly packaged with scripture (since we export most of the Gospel) means that the images that are pushed out from the top (from the USA,) are then trickled down to the nations that consume American content. The trickle-down effect is constant, and this is what contributes to stereotypes, generalizations, and ignorance of other cultures. This must also be changed.

FAKE NEWS

We have been told at church, that we shouldn't listen to or trust the mainstream media, which in evangelical language is - any news outlet that reports negative aspects of any Republican administration or the Republican party.

I've read actual comments from evangelical acquaintances who believe that the Democrats made up the hoax of the Covid-19 virus, even though in their church several members died from the same virus! The Republican conservative definition of fake news is - any news that doesn't reflect well on someone they love. In the real world however, fake news really means false news, lies. So, if a report about someone has been investigated and found to be true but that person doesn't want their story told, that isn't fake news, that's just news that you don't want others to hear.

It's another subtle form of manipulation for which many evangelicals have fallen. It's also a clear picture of totalitarianism where the expectation is that everyone must turn a deaf ear to any type of news except for what comes directly from the leader. Fear mongering is an important tactic of most if not all totalitarian regimes .... and totalitarian churches.

Once fear gets the totalitarian in office and fear hands the leader its power, it'll seem like all hell has broken loose. Under previous democratic administrations, every time something went wrong in the USA, evangelical leaders were eager to let their congregations know that the reason for these disastrous things happening in the nation was as a result of the curse that was let loose over the nation because of the non-Republican administration.

The reason for the curse was either because of the number of abortions taking place, or because the democratic government didn't do right by Israel, or simply because the Democrats now controlled the White House.

Interestingly enough in 2020 with Covid-19 running rampant all over the nation under a Republican administration, not enough personal protective equipment for healthcare personnel working through the pandemic, George Floyd's murder, marches and protests in most major cities, fires in California, earthquakes in Las Vegas, looting, riots and mayhem all over the United States, all I heard from evangelical leaders this time around was: *"Don't forget to pray for our president so that he can have wisdom to steer the nation in the right direction."*

There's nothing wrong with that prayer, it was and always is the right thing to pray. However, there was no mention of the curse taking over the nation, and no such prayers are ever prayed for democratic presidents in office. Why? The evangelical church only works with and favors Republican administrations.

WHITE ASSISTANCE

Please don't ever believe that there aren't any White people who believe in justice and equality for everyone, because there are many. I personally know some of them, they are dear friends both in and out of the Church and I am very thankful for them! After the murder of George Floyd and the ensuing protests, some of my White acquaintances reached out to me to see what they could do or how they could help, and I know that I am not the only Black person that has had that happen to them. We want you to know that we are extremely grateful.

White people should be comfortable in knowing that they won't ever completely understand the Black experience and that it's not even necessary. What is necessary however, is to speak out about injustice. We both know what's right and what's wrong.

Even with the assistance from White people that seems to be manifesting right now, Black people still need to be prepared to continue to walk this out alone if we must. Standing on the Word of God alone will not eradicate racism. If that was the case, we wouldn't be here right now. In Matthew Chapter 13 verse 15 Jesus said every plant that His heavenly Father didn't plant must be pulled up at the root. Racism must be pulled up at the root, and we must add work to our faith.

There are significant numbers of politically active evangelical conservatives who are leaders in the Church, yet who have been in agreement with every bigoted statement on Mexicans, POWs, etc. I say that they agree because they are silent about it, and I view their silence as consent. Some Black churchgoers sit in the pews watching their Pastors/Leaders with narrowed side eyes thinking: Does my Pastor know what's going on?

Why is he/she silent on these very important matters that affect the people of color and minorities in this congregation? Does he/she know that I am affected? How can they be silent during a time like this? If the Pastor/leader agrees with the racist narrative, how can he claim to care about me? Me the Mexican... Me the immigrant... Me the gay person... Me the transgender person... Me the Black person... Me!

After a while the congregant most likely, silently tiptoes out the back door never to be seen at your church again. How do we know that our church leaders aren't in favor with the racist narrative that ensued as a result of voting the way they said we should? We'll know it when they say it. If they're silent, what do they expect the minorities in their congregations to think?

I am not suggesting that any Pastor/Leader interrupt their Sunday morning service to address these issues, but then again, maybe you should! And if you feel the heart of your members, you'll make a time and a place to discuss what they are now walking through, and you will show them that you care by discussing the issues that they're facing, not in a roundabout way as in: *"If you're experiencing any challenges, here are a couple of scriptures."* That won't cut it.

Would you please sit with your congregation and say something to the effect of: *"How are you dealing with this? I am so sorry that you saw and heard this rhetoric against you and your family. Sometimes you're going to have to turn the TV off and feed your spirit with the Word. I do want to pray with you, and I want you to know that I really care about you. I care about what affects you and your family. I apologize if it seems like I didn't care. I want to make sure that you're OK. How can I help you?"*

Be prepared for their answers, because everyone isn't going to smile back at you and say that everything is OK because they are blessed and highly favored even though I'm pretty sure that some of them would. Pastors will be shocked at what they hear if they listen, and I understand that some things will be difficult to hear, but these things must be said, these discussions must be had! No longer will you be able to stand up in the pulpit as Black person after Black person gets gunned down in the streets, while you're busy preaching on the 100-fold return. There is a time and a place for everything. We're Black. We're seated in the church that you pastor. We need to hear from you.

CHURCH THEN AND NOW

There were evangelical leaders who agreed with the civil rights movement but feared retaliation and the loss of financial backing if they spoke out. So, to keep the peace they kept silent, completely disregarding the trauma of their church members in favor of the tithes and offerings they would receive. There were also many evangelical leaders who were segregationists, using their favorite scriptures to justify racism. Not all the White churches cowered though, thank God for those who didn't! Even though some backed away and sided with the racists, there were some White churches armed with faith that stood side by side with those who were fighting for equal rights. Many of the clergy who marched with Dr King were from the North.

Some in the South continued to defend racism even though they knew that it placed their Black members at a disadvantage. Efforts to dismantle white supremacy were met with fights to keep it the way it had always been.

Carolyn Renee Dupont, Assistant Professor of History at Eastern Kentucky University in Richmond, VA puts it this way:

"Most southern Christians did not regard segregation as a sin, and they resented those who criticized their "way of life". They rejected efforts from their denominations to educate them into more enlightened racial views and frequently withheld funds from agencies in the Church who advocated for equality.

They sacked pastors who embraced any aspect of the freedom struggle. They formed lay organizations to keep their churches segregated; many individual congregations adopted formal resolutions instructing their deacons to reject black worshippers. When school integration became unavoidable, white evangelicals forsook the public schools in droves in favor of new private schools sponsored by their churches."

School segregation is no more but there are still areas in the children's church ministry where we need to change some things. I'm sure you've seen the whitened skin of Jesus with blonde hair and blue eyes in pictures. Jesus, a bronze-skinned man who spoke languages from the middle east, had his image conformed to the skin tone that was 'acceptable' to the White evangelical, and these pictures have been passed down from generation to generation and are still being used in children's church and ministry even today.

It's time to change these pictures and teach our children the truth. Instead of spouting religion, pushing already marginalized folks back into a corner, and ignoring civil rights atrocities affecting members of our congregations, we could become brave and declare that righteousness and justice go hand in hand! Are you the righteousness of God in Christ? Then show me what that means, outside of confessing it every day.

How many of us can honestly say that our church leadership addressed the Charlottesville situation directly? Or the George Floyd murder? Or the Philando Castile murder? Or the Breonna Taylor murder? Maybe even in a sermon or outside of that? Loving me means you're willing to take some action on my behalf especially if you are aware of what's happening in my community.

The pulpit is such a powerful platform! Think of what would occur if your Pastor/church leader condemned racism and white supremacy, think of how far that would go in your congregation and community, especially if the church building was in an area where most of the people in the community were minorities.

Your community would know that there was someone with spiritual authority that cared about them enough to take a stand. What we do know is that our identity in Jesus Christ has not changed. Neither has Jesus, His Word, His Spirit, or His presence. We also know that since the Word of God hasn't changed, this scripture still holds true:

Colossians 3:11
King James Version (KJV)

[11] Where there is neither Greek nor Jew, circumcision nor uncircumcision, Barbarian, Scythian, bond nor free: but Christ is all, and in all.

I would hope that our roots in Christ are planted so deeply within our being, that no one and nothing can tear them away. The Gospel is the power of God and once we believe that, there's hope for us.

If you feel that racism, structural oppression and white supremacy, is only just about black people being lynched, and that it's not happening anymore, you're wrong. Maybe you can attend a SURJ meeting (google it), watch some documentaries, get on YouTube and see what they have to offer.

As your Black brothers and sisters in Christ are suffering, there's a lot more that can be done. Keep in mind that everyone didn't start out in life on the same level, with the same provision, and the same benefits.

IT JUST TAKES ONE

There will always be those who risk or lose their lives for the sake of the whole. There will always be a Dr. Martin Luther King Jr. and a Colin Kaepernick. Even in individual families every family has at least one good rebel.

There will always be that one person who moves away from the status-quo and presses against what seems to be the norm because in their opinion, it's wrong. That courageous person could be you, but if not, maybe it's someone sitting in your pew. There's always a brave someone in every group!

I'm sure that during the era of slavery there were brave and courageous slaves who decided that since they were probably going to end up dying anyway, they would just do whatever it took in order to escape. I'm also sure that it didn't last because they were always overpowered, as those who were determined to fight back were immediately killed before they could gain some type of momentum.

At the time of the Underground Railroad even though the weapons of the slaves were nothing compared to those of their captors, many of them still tried to push through! Someone decided that slavery was wrong and decided to do whatever was necessary to cause change.

Rising up against oppression is a natural instinct, but if your oppressors can kill you without ever having to pay the price for your murder, then you sometimes just learn to adjust your life and try to ignore the oppression.

However, one day... The pent-up rage will explode. We don't need Christianity or faith to know what is right and what is wrong when it comes to how different people groups are treated. Instinctively, we know when the treatment we are handing out to someone is wrong. We know when we're being kind, and when we're being ugly.

When social media exposes racists and their behavior and these people have their feet held to the fire and accountability is demanded, the racist always tries to let their audience know that that is not really who they are, but we don't buy it.

The same thing is always said about the United States of America when acts of bigotry and racism end up on national TV, *'This is not who America is'*. Except, this is exactly who America as a country is, and has been for a very long time! If we need Christianity or faith to show us that racism is wrong, then Satan has already taken huge ground in our churches.

Dr. Martin Luther King Jr. wrote from the Birmingham jail about White southern ministers who refused to support the civil rights movement. It seemed that they saw the concerns of Black Americans as social issues, not gospel issues. There are parallels between the attitudes of the church back then toward social justice, and the attitude that persists today.

Even Dr. Martin Luther King Jr asked: *"Who is the God that these people serve?"* In Hebrews 12:26 (The Passion Translation) God said that He would shake the systems of this world and the unseen powers in the heavenly realm.

Hebrews 12:26-28
The Passion Translation (TPT)

[26] The earth was rocked at the sound of his voice from the mountain, but now he has promised,
"Once and for all I will not only shake the systems of the world,[a]
but also the unseen powers in the heavenly realm!"[b]

The system of racism is one system that will be shaken down by God, the shaking has already begun. There are many churches today filled with racists, but as the Body of Christ continues to be enlightened, hopefully we will see the error of our ways. There has already been an exodus of people out of our churches and even though I don't advocate immediately leaving a church because you don't like what's going on, I can certainly understand why it happens especially if you're experiencing racism.

TALKING ABOUT SLAVERY

The notion that remembering or talking about slavery causes division is one of the biggest lies I've heard. Does remembering the Holocaust, or remembering 9/11 cause division? Of course not! So why is it not the same way when it comes to slavery?

It's not the remembering that causes division, it's the refusal to address it for what it really was.

Slavery was an act of terrorism. There is no dispute when it comes to remembering the Holocaust and 9/11 because we can all condemn the actions of terrorists. However, when it comes to raping and beating slaves, terrorizing them, stealing and selling their children, working them halfway to death, lynching them, and getting free labor for hundreds of years, suddenly a lot of white excuses collectively rise to the surface: Black people are given reasons why remembering our history of slavery causes division, and more reasons why we should ignore the terror and horror of those tragedies, reasons why the Bible said we should forgive and forget, and we're also reminded that since this happened hundreds of years ago and we weren't there, we should just, 'Get over it'.

The narrow conservative 'get over slavery' crowd clearly can't understand how spiritual things work as they've not yet realized that the spirit of racism is still comfortably ensconced above this nation, pulling the strings of people in places of authority over this nation, including evangelical leadership.

On the Richter scale of life this is huge. Systemic racism caused a great divide. Even though it is correct to say that White people who are alive right now had nothing to do with slavery, the same White people that are alive right now continue to enjoy the benefits of slavery that their ancestors created on the backs of Black people, without lending a voice to the Black cause. If you're Black I'm sure you've either heard this phrase or it was spoken to you regarding slavery, *"No White person alive owned slaves, and no Black person alive was a slave, don't expect me to pay for something I didn't do."* This is usually a line of defense when Black people speak out about their own Black lives. Firstly, no one is asking anyone to pay for what their ancestors did. We just want to live as freely as White people do.

It's as simple as that. The generational wealth that was passed down because of slavery, as well as systemic racism and Jim Crow are the main things that enable White people to live a much more different life than most Black people, and still, some don't even want us to voice that our lives matter? Ridiculous!

If the Black community's history of enslavement makes you uncomfortable, or if you're reading this and thinking that I have totally lost my mind, it's quite possibly that you're seeing things through the lens of white privilege which doesn't allow for empathy. There may be a bit of discomfort, but these stories deserve to be told. I am hopeful that every day

Black people will continue to overcome being stigmatized, over-penalized, and marginalized.

I do also fully expect that the Body of Christ can and will change from its racist roots. Even though we've already alienated many hopefuls and people groups, and many who love Jesus and His Word have chosen to worship and fellowship by themselves at home, it doesn't have to be that way. Those who left 'church as usual' to worship at home will soon find out that the church they left is now working on dismantling structural racism in the pews, and that 'church as usual' has become a thing of the past, glory hallelujah!

BLACK POWER

There is a slow yet steady rising percentage of Black people who have learned how to operate as the wealthy do despite the obstacles in their pathway. What that means, is that the rules are about to be changed for the earthly powers that be whose intention was to keep the system of wealth just as it has always been, with zero access to wealth for those who aren't White.

We currently measure the economy by how well rich White people are doing (by looking at Wall Street and the stock market), but that method doesn't give the true picture of how everyone else is in the nation is doing.

How Wall Street is doing doesn't affect people who have no 401Ks and nothing in the stock market! There should be another way to measure the economy. Most Black people grew up hearing that they should study twice as hard, work twice as hard, and jump twice as high to achieve what easily falls into the lap of a White person. Many, who work and jump twice as much, have still bumped into the wall of systemic racism, but there are some that have found that some of those barriers can be broken but it's a real hard fight, a tough hill to climb.

It shouldn't have to be this way though, since it's not that way for everyone. Withstanding the oppression and micro-aggressions that accompany racism and doing it authentically, is no easy feat. But if you're doing it unashamed of who you are, what shade of Black your skin is, whether your hair curl pattern is 3B or 4C, and whether you're a size 6 or size 22, more power to you, I am proud of you!

The history of Black people being bought and sold for financial gain, continues even to this day, as Black men/women are imprisoned more than any other race, and for-profit prisons are all the rage. The United States is the world leader in incarceration, and we all know that all Americans are not incarcerated equally. In many instances, the same crime was committed, both men/women had no prior history of crime, but both received different sentences based on the color of their skin.

A White person even though committing the same crime as a Black person, will end up with probation. For the Black person however, there will most likely be a prison sentence. This is the real *'stop the steal'* that needs to be addressed. Stop stealing Black lives! Stop stealing Black futures! Stop stealing Black energy! Stop stealing Black money! Stop stealing from Black people, enough is enough! This is terrorism that has been unchallenged for too long.

All the talk about Black power that angers some, and causes others to fear, isn't really what it's made out to be. Black power is the power we possess when we're acting together as one. Black power is being aware of the racial system of injustice that is standing against us, being used by some to oppress; yet still choosing to believe that together with your Black brothers and sisters, you have already overcome with the Word of God, the Spirit of God, and the Blood of Jesus.

Where you and I are right now requires that we walk through what Jesus has already paid for, all the while remaining steady and resilient. Black power, the power of the people as one, is spiritual power, political power, and activist power. It is also social and financial power. Black dollars matter and business owners know this! What would happen if Black people stopped buying from anyone else except Black owned businesses? The American economy will suffer.

Black power doesn't hide in the closets of life, a-praying and a-hoping for a change that may or may not come in our lifetime. Black power is taking that prayer power out of the closet and into the community, adding works to our faith.

Black power is knowing that even though other people groups say that some Black people are being troublesome and that we cause division, we keep going. I can tell you right now that I have no intention of stopping; I have been called to this assignment!

I read this paragraph last night, that some attribute to Harriet Tubman:

> "If you hear the dogs, keep going. If you see the torches in the woods, keep going. If there's shouting after you keep going. Don't ever stop. Keep going. If you want a taste of freedom, keep going."

As you keep going, that is Black power. You must keep going, because the ancestors of other communities weren't dealt with like those of your community were.

Therefore, press on you must! Heaven is cheering you on, your ancestors are cheering you on! Press on! Press with the Black power, Black resilience, Black fortitude, Black backbone, Black strength and Black joy that you *know* belongs to you.

There was blood spilled on your behalf.

Press on Black one, press on!

"Negroes

Sweet and docile

Meek humble and kind

Beware the day

They change their minds!

Wind in the cotton fields

Gentle breeze

Beware the hour

It uproots trees!"

(By: Langston Hughes)

Chapter 6

THE CONSERVATIVE PRO-LIFER

HIGHLIGHTING BLACK WOMEN:

TARIKA WILSON was a 26-year-old woman who was shot and killed when a Lima, Ohio Police SWAT team raided her home to arrest her boyfriend. She had her youngest son Sincere, in her arms when she was shot. Sincere, who was 14 months old, was shot in the shoulder and hand but survived.

The officer was acquitted of the misdemeanor charges of negligent homicide and negligent assault. He testified that he felt his life was in danger when he shot her and that he saw a shadow and heard gunshots nearby; but they actually came from officers, downstairs. Rest in peace and power, Tarika!

Pro-life... That means all life and not just those that are still in the womb, right? In evangelical camps their life's mission is to make sure not another baby is murdered in its mother's womb. Pro-choice... This is not a blanket support of abortion; it's a statement that denies the government the right to make a mother's decision for her. Being pro-birth doesn't make you righteous; righteousness comes from faith in Jesus Christ.

God cares for those in the womb, and He cares for those outside of the womb. There are Christians who believe that being pro-choice is OK, and that we should leave women alone to make their own decisions. Then there are Christians that believe that people who are pro-choice are angering God and are going to hell.

Abortion isn't something that I would personally recommend to anyone, and I'm also not going to Bible-thump and brow-beat someone because they plan on having an abortion, when I can share wisdom with them, and options, and certainly cover the person with prayer.

Anything that has to do with killing, stealing, or destroying is a consequence of the fall of man in the Garden of Eden but the way that abortion has been defined as the one thing that makes it or breaks it for the conservative Republican vote is sad. It has created single-issue voting (which is what it was designed to do) and it has also created single-issue evangelicalism which is unhealthy.

As we discussed in previous chapters, it is our deep need to separate ourselves from others who don't look like us, believe like us, think like us, dress like us, worship like us, pray like us, sing like us and live like us, coupled with our inability to embrace each other's differences, that caused the divide we see today in the Church. We somehow feel the need to make it very clear to the other camps that we proudly wear the Pro-Life label, and they don't. We insist on magnifying our differences, but again, this is the narrowest way to live.

I've heard different things in the Church on both sides of the aisle concerning abortion. *"I am Pro-choice, and you can't tell me how to vote."* Or *"I am Pro-life and as long as the candidate is Pro-life, I refuse to vote any other way."* It would be cool if we could co-exist with our beliefs, but so far that's not been the case.

The typical Pro-lifer believes that life begins at conception and many of these same people really do not care about the baby after the child is born. The focus is that the woman does not abort, then all is well. That's a pretty good argument when your focus is not really life, but anti-abortion.

This is how I see it: Pro-life includes wanting life for every person, from the time the person is born to the time they die. Pro-life includes everyone's lives and not just lives that you deem to be worthy. How could Pro-life not include the poor and marginalized? Aren't those lives as well? What about those with disabilities?

Or those of the LGBTQ community? Or Black and Brown immigrants? If we are fighting for the lives within the womb then let us also continue the fight for them when they are out of the womb and grown. These are real children, women, men, families.

A comment I read once on social media said that at this point, we're not Pro-life, we are pro-fetus. I agree. I saw this posted on social media just before the 2016 elections: *"If you stand on the Democratic platform, you support killing babies."* It's not just this one gentleman that posted it, millions of evangelicals feel the same way.

I so badly wanted to be a petty Betty and respond with: *"And since you stand on the Republican platform, you support grabbing women by their genitals."* (I didn't respond to his comment because this is as narrow minded and depthless as they come, and I would have been buying into the rhetoric). My point is that it's this type of narrative that helps to deepen the divide in the Church.

It is amazing to listen to Pro-lifers, who stand up strong against abortion (as they should, since this the label they choose to be identified by), because they place great value on human lives. Is it the belief of some that the women who have abortions, have less rights than those that don't have abortions?

Do they believe that the lives of those of the LGBTQ community, Muslims, and people of color are worth less than other lives?

This isn't an either/or situation, it isn't an all or none situation either. We can be Pro-life and have love for immigrants, single moms and minorities who have had abortions as well. The Church isn't here to win arguments because in the process we end up losing our influence. We maintain and keep our influence by using Jesus as our role model, by loving people, showing them that we care.

Our views on abortion shouldn't be pushed on others to show everyone that we are of the conservative persuasion. That may gain us more social media likes from others who think like we do, but very few will want us to share our Jesus with them.

If we've adopted the label of either Pro-life or Pro-choice, we have chosen to be identified in a certain way, and this chosen label screams at the world louder than the word 'Christian' does! Every label does that. Every label divides and isolates people groups; the Church should not be the body of people leading the way with labels and division.

ABORTION AND GOD'S PURPOSES IN THE EARTH

I was having a conversation with someone about abortion, and she explained her views to me in this way: *"Do Christians think that we're that smart to deny a purpose or a life from coming into the earth? Are we God? The purpose that was terminated when the baby's life was terminated, don't you think that that life/purpose can re-enter the earth?*

> *That life/purpose can come right back into the earth in another package. You know how I know that's possible? Because it is God Who places His purposes in our hearts. With God all things are possible. He knows the perfect time for everyone to be born."*

I understand and I believe what she said. Just as God had William Seymour, Mother Teresa, and Bishop T D Jakes on the earth at the perfect time to fulfil their purposes, I believe that it's the same thing for anyone including the babies.

She also said:

"Let's change our thinking for a moment and put God's purpose front and center. God's purpose must be fulfilled in the earth at the right time.

The baby may be gone because he/she was aborted, but the purpose of God still lives on in spiritual realms, and that purpose can never ever be aborted.

There are certain things that are supposed to happen in the earth at certain times, people that are to be born at certain times, and no amount of prayer and confessions can bring them to pass before that time comes."

I am not making light of the children who are no longer with us because of abortion, but I am trying to get the Church to stop looking at this as an either/or situation based on the labels we have assumed. Look at this in a different way. Yes, they are precious lives, but the labels that we cling to so fearfully have us living such narrow lives that we're unable to think outside of the limited space we've created for ourselves. Do you agree that with every person born there is purpose attached? Do you believe that God has a plan for every person?

What happens if someone lives their entire life then dies without knowing what their purpose was for being alive? What if that dead person's purpose was to preach the gospel but they never tapped into it?

What if, before the foundation of the world God determined that he would need 3 million preachers to be actively preaching the gospel of Grace in the year 2022, and this person that died was supposed to be one of the preachers, but didn't know it?

Would God sit around wringing His hands trying to figure out what to do? Of course not! This has all been mapped out already by the Creator of the universe and God knows how to get someone else to fill that person's place to get His purpose in the earth. God's purpose will never die! Maybe there is a mother who aborted her baby; the purpose that was attached to the aborted baby didn't die with the baby.

There is someone else alive (many people, actually) who wants to have a baby! The Purpose of God for the aborted baby will have another chance to re-enter the earth through someone who really wants to have a baby and has no plans to abort the child. This in no way diminishes the horrors of abortion or the life of the baby.

We may be able to access God's power to live and to change our lives, and we can tread on serpents and scorpions and over all the power of the enemy, but when it comes to determining the purpose of God or stopping the purpose of God, we're simply just not that powerful. God's purposes for mankind shall come to pass.

CHOOSING LIFE IS A CHOICE – OUR CHOICE

We can be Pro-life without dictating what others should choose. Adding works to our faith in this situation doesn't mean that we go stand outside the abortion clinic screaming at everyone that approaches the building.

Even God didn't choose life for us, He gave us the choice,

"Choose life that you and your descendants may live!"

Deuteronomy 30:19
New King James Version (KJV)

[19] I call heaven and earth as witnesses today against you, *that* I have set before you, life and death, blessing and cursing; therefore, choose life, that both you and your descendants may live.

He wants life for us, but it is still a choice. It is *our* choice! He wants us to be saved, but it's also *our* choice. No Christian reading this book was forced into salvation, you made the choice yourself! Just as we pray for others to be saved, we should be praying that there are suitable avenues and solutions for women who feel like they don't want to have their babies. But to stand in front of the abortion clinic with handheld signs as we yell and scream at the women going into the clinic, that doesn't help our cause.

In a 2008 article by the Society for the Protection of Unborn Children, I read: *"Abortion has killed more Black people than the Ku Klux Klan."* And on a 2020 social media post I read something similar that came from a Pastor: *"Abortion kills more Black lives in 2 weeks than the Ku Klux Klan did in all of its existence combined.*

So the same people who are screaming 'Black Lives Matter,' are screaming: "More abortion, more abortion, more abortion." Whew!

There are so many different directions I could go with those two statements, but I won't. The second statement spoken by a Pastor at a church is even more disturbing when you realize that white church leadership spewed these racist words to a congregation without being challenged!

We've hit an all-time low. What in the world has this congregation been taught so that this racist narrative is okay with them? Pastor, if you don't understand what Black Lives Matter is about, please be silent.

Here are the stats about abortion according to 2017 statistics from a Pro-Lifer's study:

- 39% of abortion patients were white women
- 28% were Black women
- 25% were Hispanic women
- 8% were women of other races
- 27% were women aged 25-29
- 8% were women between the ages of 18-19
- 58% of abortion patients were Christians! (Read that one twice!) Here's the breakdown:
- 17% Protestants

- 13% Evangelicals
- 24% Catholics
- 8% Other
- 38% claimed "no religious affiliation."

Focus on the Family in a 2018 article entitled: *Survey – Women Go Silently From Church to Abortion Clinic,* states that 4 in 10 women who have had abortions are Christian women who are convinced that the Church would rather gossip than help them. The same article says that among women who have had an abortion:

- Two-thirds (65 percent) say church members judge single women who are pregnant.
- A majority (54 percent) think churches oversimplify decisions about pregnancy options.
- Fewer than half (41 percent) believe churches are prepared to help with decisions about unwanted pregnancies.
- Only three in 10 think churches give accurate advice about pregnancy options.

THE SINGLE ISSUE IS ABORTION

Many conservative evangelicals are single issue voters. That issue is abortion. What would Jesus do about abortion? Well, in our minds, He would send them all to hell, those who performed the abortions, and those who had their babies aborted. We have preached morality for decades, but it was convenient to turn a blind eye at the divisive tone of the Trump administration simply because they espoused anti-abortion views. Forget about morality and living according to the Word, *"we're not electing a Pastor, we're electing a president*!" And that is true.

In the two last elections before 2016, some congregations were blamed by their leadership for the *'mistake'* that was made with the last non-republican president in office, sigh. It is essential for the conservative evangelical leader to rally the evangelical troops to vote for the republican nominee who is not in favor of abortion. I heard someone say (and I agree with her) that evangelical leaders were attempting to use the single issue of abortion in order to get the Church to vote for racism. In other words: He's a racist, but the more important thing is that he is anti-abortion, so come on Church let's all cast our votes for him!

PRO-LIFERS AND THE LGBTQ COMMUNITY

What is so frustrating to me is that some of us will go out of our way to make people who don't live or behave like us miserable. The dislike of and sometimes even the hatred directed towards the LGBTQ community is un-Christ-like. Our love for each other and our love for Jesus should be the defining factor when dealing with anyone who doesn't behave like we think they should!

Instead of loving others, we have agreed with the narrowness of conservatism which has, as we've seen from previous chapters, created yet another row of division.

In my research for this book, I was surprised to discover that violence against the LGBTQ community has increased in the last 3 years.

According to the Human Rights Campaign, there were 37 transgender murders in 2020 in the United States and according to Forbes there were 350 transgender murders globally in 2020 as well. Elinor Aspegren of USA Today in an article on July 9, 2020 wrote:

"The Human Rights Campaign has been tracking transgender homicides since 2013. This year is worse than all of them so far. At least four transgender people have been murdered in the past week, including at least three Black transgender women, bringing the HRC's yearly count to 21 – nearly matching 2019's total of 27.

The organization has never seen such a high number at this point in the year, and other advocates across the U.S. are horrified by the rampant and repeated murders. Bree Black, a 27-year-old Black transgender woman, was found fatally shot July 3 in Pompano Beach, Florida. Summer Taylor, a 24-year-old white non-binary person, was fatally struck by a vehicle July 4 while they were participating in the Black Femme March in Seattle.

Merci Mack, a 22-year-old Black transgender woman was found fatally shot on June 30 in Dallas. The next day, 32-year-old Black transgender woman, Shakie Peters was killed in Amite City, Louisiana. The deaths of two other Black transgender women, one in Baton Rouge, Louisiana, and another in Philadelphia, remain under investigation, according to advocacy groups."

"It is ridiculous that we have to continue to hash-tag our friends' names and add them to a list of names to be memorialized every year, and that we expect it," Carter Brown, Executive Director of National Black Trans Advocacy Coalition, told USA TODAY."

He added, "We expect it because too many trans women of color are continuously being murdered and beaten with minimum or no consequence being brought to the assailants."

The hatred directed towards this community isn't just coming from the world; it comes from the Church as well. Many of the LGBTQ community grew up in Christian homes and have been ostracized by their own family members! That of course often leads to unemployment, eviction, chronic homelessness, sickness and yes… even their own death.

It's almost laughable that the same evangelicals who protested unisex bathrooms because of the likelihood of their children being sexually molested while using public bathrooms, are some of the same evangelicals who encouraged their congregations to vote for the Republican nominee in the 2016 elections!

The hypocrisy is astounding. Is it possible that both the evangelical Republicans and the evangelical Democrats might have ideas on both sides of the fence that they can all agree with?

That will take some really 'outside-the-box-we've-created-for-ourselves' thinking, but nothing is impossible with God! Until we get there, let's not forget that there is something to be said for creating a church culture that has the love of Jesus at its heart.

If the love of Jesus isn't present, then Jesus won't be promoted in our churches. Instead, we'll end up promoting one of the kingdoms of this world maybe the Republican kingdom or the Democratic kingdom.

Even if that happens, I believe that there is hope yet. There is always hope because the Bible has everything covered!

Revelation 11:15
King James Version (KJV)

And the seventh angel sounded; and there were great voices in heaven, saying, "The kingdoms of this world are become the kingdoms of our Lord, and of his Christ; and he shall reign forever and ever."

The kingdoms of this world will all eventually become the kingdoms of our God and of His Christ, and Jesus will reign forever and ever! Until that great kingdom exchange occurs, let's learn to reflectively listen, listen with the intent to shower people with the love of God. The only thing that anyone should receive when they visit our churches should be Jesus, His Word and His Love, rather than snippets of our adulterous affairs with various party platforms.

Jesus would not have aligned Himself with the Republican platform! Let me say it this way: **Jesus would not have aligned Himself with any political party, He is not a politician.** That's the teaching that caused us to lose our way and our witness, as well as several thousand members in the process. **God didn't send us His only begotten Son to stick it to the LGBTQ community or any community. Yet here we are!**

I listened as a Pastor described how she walked into the sanctuary of her church building and said hello to a few people who showed up early for the service. She said that as she was walking down the aisle, she looked across the sanctuary and saw a gay couple walk in (if I'm remembering correctly, she said they were holding hands). The couple walked through the pews and got a seat, but two parishioners sitting in that row took one look at the gay couple, got up and changed their seats. She said she was shocked, and her heart sank when she realized that people in the church that she pastored with her husband would act that way to visitors at their church.

That behavior is on display more times than we realize, and that's why many of the LGBTQ community wouldn't come to visit our churches even if we paid them to, and I don't blame them for it. Attempting to show the LGBTQ community the 'error of their ways' and trying to change their community into *our* image and likeness, causes further friction.

THE PRO-LIFER AND IMMIGRATION

Even if you don't read the Bible and you don't believe in God, helping people that are in need is simply being a good human being. I was happy to read about the churches that showed up at the Mexican border to help those who were in need as caravans of people attempted to cross the borders into the United States.

I love it when the Church can step in and help wherever we are needed, without debating about who should be here in the United States and who shouldn't, mostly based on the color of their skin or what their country of origin was. This is a nation of immigrants.

The majority of those at the border are desperate people who walked for thousands of miles to get here for help. Who would want to do that except for the fact that they were really desperate? I don't think they took the long trek because they want to come to the United States to rape your daughter or steal your gun, do you?

We could put our heads together as the Church and have answers and viable solutions for those that need us. If we all could ever get together outside of divisive camps and denominations, I'm sure that we'll see that the spiritual capacity among us is huge!

We could at least give it a try! I sincerely hope that some of us aren't silent about border issues because these immigrants don't look like us. What if most of immigrants at the border are hard-working families who see an opportunity to escape extreme poverty and have a better life?

I'm pretty sure that if we put ourselves in their shoes, and we were poor, hungry, and tired; we won't ever stop trying to get to a better life, especially for our children. For sure, the United States is unable to accommodate everyone that shows up at our borders, but we can be humane and compassionate with those we meet. That's the least we can do. Mobilizing efforts to go to the border to help those in need or sending resources to churches that are close to the border, will manifest in signs and wonders for those needing help.

I know that some churches that were in the vicinity of the border showed up with food, water, clothing and whatever else was necessary to welcome them and that makes my heart sing! When scripture is used to measure who should come in and who should stay out of the country, it completely misses the entire point because the God that I know would welcome all of those whom some of us would like to see remain on the outside.

Psalms 2:8
The Passion Translation (TPT)

Ask Me to give you the nations and I will do it,
and they shall become your legacy.
Your domain will stretch to the ends of the earth.

It's interesting to me that we've been praying Psalms 2:8 for decades in the Church. We have asked God to send us those who don't know Him, we've asked Him to give us the nations. Then He sends the nations to us, except they're at the southern border and they're not the color we anticipated. Uh oh, what do we do now?

"No, no, no God! Send others of a different color, send those from white nations instead, please!" Church, we're going to have to love our neighbor, regardless of where they were born. One of the reasons I believe that churches are growing in leaps and bounds

outside the USA, is because those countries don't have many of the privileges that American churches have, and they are solely depending on God and God alone.

American evangelicals don't have to walk several miles to get to church and we don't have to trudge through mud to get to church either. As a matter of fact, in the United States if there's mud on the streets then that's the perfect reason to skip out on going to church! The American church has options that many other nations don't.

THE GOVERNMENT SHALL BE UPON HIS SHOULDER

The Bible says that the Government should be upon the shoulders of the Body of Christ.

Isaiah 9:6
King James Version (KJV)

[6] For unto us a child is born, unto us a son is given: and the government shall be upon his shoulder: and his name shall be called Wonderful, Counsellor, The mighty God, The everlasting Father, The Prince of Peace.

We are the body of Christ, the shoulder is on the body, and the Government should be carried by us, on our shoulders. This means that some of the things we're expecting the Government to do, for example, taking care of the poor and needy - should be done by the church, but we got so caught up in believing for bigger houses and cars that taking care of those in need became somewhat of an inconvenience.

What I'm seeing is that the Government is not on the shoulders of the body of Christ, because we've expertly decided that it was much better and smarter to not just carry the Government, but to marry the Government. If the right party ended up in power, there would be a marriage between that party and the Church!

If we believe that immigrants are the cause of America's problems, we're wrong. We can't repeat the same fear-based information that the world does concerning immigrants, especially when we already know where fear comes from!

We can't blame anyone for the issues our churches face, because when we do, that keeps us from noticing the main reason we're having hard times in the Church: we've adopted labels that have narrowed our sphere of influence and severely weakened our impact.

Chapter 7

MISOGYNY & SEXUAL ABUSE IN THE CHURCH

HIGHLIGHTING BLACK WOMEN:

TYIANNA ALEXANDER was a 28-year-old trans-gender woman who was killed in Chicago by a gunshot to her head on January 6, 2021. No-one has been charged with her murder. Rest in peace and power Tyianna!

There is a culture of misogyny and sexual abuse that has been simmering in some churches and major corporations alike and provides a sliver of understanding of how these things work in such places. Joy-Ann Reid, host of MSNBC's The Reid Out on her Twitter account 4-3-2017 said this: *"The Ailes-O'Reilly scandal & the apparent culture at Fox News clarifies why their viewers were 'meh' on Trump's teen peeping/grabby vulgarity."* She's right!

If this is standard behavior in major corporations, why would anyone in a leadership position move towards making changes? Could it be that it's the same for the Church? That everything is okay because we've covered up enough sexual abuse situations and we would prefer to keep it that way?

Or could it be that the Church has forgiven the perpetrator and wishes to no longer talk about the issue while said perpetrator remains on staff? When the same conservative spiritual leaders who condemned Bill Clinton's infidelity, came to Donald Trump's defense after the leaking of the Access Hollywood tape in 2016, there was very little left to discern. There was grace and forgiveness for the Republican candidate, but not for the Democratic candidate.

I remember sitting at a church service many years ago when an evangelical leader was condemning Bill Clinton based on his exceptionally poor behavior in the White House but for some reason, I can't seem to find many of the Christian leadership who were willing to stand in their pulpits and say something similar about President Trump. Condemning anyone is wrong, but I think I may know why it occurred for one president and not for the other.

SEXUAL ABUSE

There are far more churches concerned with the rehabbing of the perpetrators of sexual abuse while simultaneously neglecting the victims. I am not sure why church leadership naturally tends to gravitate towards the abuser while at the same time heaping shame upon the victim. Of course, this isn't every church, but it has happened more times than it should.

I am all for the rehabilitation of both parties, but once a crime has been committed; standing the abuser in the pulpit to inform us that they have repented doesn't do much to help the victim. I don't believe that rehabilitation for the abuser should be done at the expense of the victim. Minimizing the abuse has the effect of shoving it up under the carpet, which then also paves the way for more abuse in the Church. Our churches should be a place where those who were abused are welcomed and made to feel safe. They should know that once they walk through the doors of our sanctuaries, they're at home. Our church members need to be made aware, that the Church will stand by them if something as horrible as sexual abuse occurs, especially if it happens to them or to their children while in the church building.

In abusive marriages, the abused spouse needs to know that his/her church is a safe environment as well. We can pray in tongues all we want to, that still doesn't change the fact that we're in a fallen world and things happen. It can and will however, change the extent to which things happen, but let's not forget that everyone isn't on the same spiritual ground and that we are our brother's keeper.

Churches need a plan in place for sexual abuse. I know that background checks are conducted for staff and volunteers but that doesn't mean that those in the church leadership know everything and everyone. If Katie is sexually abused by an Elder, what happens then? Then there's Shameeka. What if she is also sexually abused by a Pastor? Will she receive the same or different treatment than Katie?

There should be an open-door policy for sexual abuse allegations, as well as proper investigations and appropriate action must be taken. I once heard a national discussion about attempted rape, but it was referred to as a *'youthful indiscretion'*. When will some men realize that violence against women is unacceptable? Scripture has been misinterpreted and wrongly divided to justify misogyny and sexism and we must put a stop to it! Why aren't more women believed when they speak out against it?

The idea of not believing the voices of women goes all the way back to Bible days. If you read Luke Chapter 23, verses 55-56, as well as Luke Chapter 24, verses 1-11 you'll see the story of Mary Magdalene, Joanna, and Mary the mother of James who visited the tomb and saw Jesus' body there.

They prepared ointments and spices then went back to the tomb but encountered angels there who told them that Jesus wasn't there anymore. The women left; went back to the apostles to tell them what the angels said about Jesus, but those men didn't believe the women either!

Luke 24:11
Good News Translation (GNT)

But the apostles thought that what the women said was nonsense, and they did not believe them.

At the very core of narrow conservatism there's a group of evangelicals acknowledging Jesus by mouth yet denying Him in other areas. Stressing the importance of family values yet drawing comparisons to the Bible story of Mary and Joseph when faced with questions about sexual abuse in the Church.

CONSERVATISM AND THE ME-TOO MOVEMENT

The Me-Too movement has been said to have given voices to women, but we have always had voices and for the most part we've always used them. One of the reasons that it seems like we're just now using our voices is that social media platforms allow for millions of people on any given day to share situations of abuse and injustice against women which then almost forces the media to pick up on these issues, or the ones that they deem worthy to be shared on their network.

There are more people watching and listening to the stories of women and some men, which has led to once powerful men being held accountable in the Church, and in the private sector. In some instances, there have been resignations, but there are also those who have denied the accusations of the women.

Some of the men have been accused by as many as 9, 14 and even 19 different women of sexual abuse! The defamation and silencing of women are being brought to the forefront of discussions; and the growing number of sexual misconduct scandals surrounding people in high places could be one reason for the large female interest in political activism.

Women are continuing to rise, ready to share their experiences of sexual abuse and rape which sometimes leads to man-made kingdoms toppling down. The influence of these women will most certainly continue to grow even in conservative states.

The massive shift that has taken place with the 'Me-Too' movement is here to stay. One can only hope that there is now in place a new, higher state of demeanor regarding the behavior of men in power and that they will realize that the sense of entitlement they have previously held regarding women's bodies could now bring them face to face with a prison sentence.

PASTOR MAY I PLEASE?

Why should women have to change their dress code and cover up their armpits just because some evangelical men don't know how to behave? If a woman's armpits cause these men to become excited as they're preaching in the pulpit, I'd say there's a freak or two hanging out with the Pastor. An armpit, really?

Depending on where you attend church, some women still aren't allowed to teach or minister. They're also not allowed to wear sleeveless dresses, pants, and in some cases, they also aren't allowed to wear makeup!

Yet, despite the churches that still have these rules wrapped up in Old Testament scripture; women are freer now than we've ever been. We watch as some men are being upended from their comfy seats as misogyny is being forced to bow in the Church.

Some churches have yet to have a woman ordained as a Pastor, although ordination is not necessary for anyone to preach.

Women have been frustrated with the status quo at churches, where we continuously were relegated to leadership positions that have traditionally been held by women: pianist, nursery director, choir director, children's ministry director etc. Look at the staff on the websites of some of the largest churches in America and you'll find that their leadership positions are filled with men (except for the traditionally held leadership positions for women).

Despite this, there is a rising tide of women in ministry who are no longer waiting on *'approval'* from their male counterparts to do what God has called them to do. The lack of a *'spiritual covering'* that we've been told we needed to have in order to be in ministry, isn't holding these women back!

The timing couldn't have been any better for the long-awaited grace-based teaching on Gender Roles. It's a teaching we never knew we needed until it arrived on the scene, and it has been embraced by free women everywhere! More women are poised to lead in more areas than ever in the body of Christ because of the revelation of Gender Roles. I'm thankful!

MISOGYNY AND PATRIARCHY

If you are a woman who is standing up to patriarchy, I'm sure you've sensed intimidation, but my advice to you is to keep on pressing. Women who take a stand against patriarchy and misogyny are always deemed to either be prudish, whorish, unprofessional, unattractive, hysterical, or extremely sensitive. There will always be something said about a Christian woman (or any woman) who is disrupting the male evangelical status quo. There will also be presumptions made about how much we weigh, how many times we've failed, and why we're still single. This all goes to show how disposable some women really are to so many men. Keep it moving, sis!

Misogyny in the Church is just as much a business as racism is in America. It's a for profit business at that. I don't believe that my gender affects my spirituality in a negative way, but that's the way some see it. Jesus stood up for the equality of both men and women, and He honored women when it was taboo! Remember the woman caught in adultery? (John 8:1-11). Or Mary being the first to see the empty tomb? (John 20:11-18). Or the woman at the well? (John 4:7-26). Or the woman with the alabaster perfume bottle? (Mark 14:3-9).

We're bound to have extremists and hijackers of good causes, but that doesn't mean that we sit back and act like misogyny and sexism isn't happening in our churches. Women matter, our voices matter, and our stories matter.

Chapter 8

PROSPERITY & THE CONSERVATIVE EVANGELICAL

HIGHLIGHTING BLACK WOMEN:

FELYCYA HARRIS was a 33-year-old transgender woman who was found shot dead in a park in Augusta, Georgia. Her death was ruled a homicide, but no one has been charged with her murder. Rest in peace and power, Felycya!

Sharing the Gospel from a privileged western perspective can sometimes come off as unappealing, especially when the focus is on prosperity. Even with scripture to back it up, there are many who are offended by the preaching of prosperity, and I believe I know why.

The prosperity of God's people can be found all over the Old Testament, with Solomon operating in a level of wealth and wisdom that had never been seen before.

We know that it is God Who gives us the power to get wealth because He has a plan for it: to establish His covenant in the earth!

Deuteronomy 8:18
New King James Version (NKJV)

[18] "And you shall remember
the LORD your God, for *it is* He who
gives you power to get wealth, that He
may [a]establish His covenant which He
swore to your fathers, as *it is* this day.

We can also see that God's Blessing makes us rich, without sorrow.

I like to call that, #WealthyWithoutMess.

Proverbs 10:22
New King James Version (NKJV)

[22] The blessing of the LORD makes one rich,
And He adds no sorrow with it.

We are always going to need Jesus whether we're prosperous or not, prosperity certainly is the will of God! But what do you do when there are no answers to your prayers, no manifestation from the tithes and offerings you've given, and no results from the scriptures you've been quoting?

One major thing to continue doing is exactly what Jesus said to do in Mark 11:22, *"Have faith in God."* Your answers will come, and manifestations shall occur; things don't always happen overnight. In the meantime, help should still be made available to you and your family. I believe that every church should have a Benevolent Department, but unfortunately, not all do. For those that do, because the needs of the congregation are usually so great, sometimes churches run out of money in their benevolent fund during the first week of the month.

What's a family in need to do then? The narrow conservative way of thinking permeates some churches to the point where congregants are policed over their giving, church attendance, and unpaid (volunteer) service. I know of someone who went to her church to ask for help to get food years ago and sat for an interview with one of the Pastors on staff. He asked if she was a tither and then pulled up her tithing record as she sat there!

He used the records to show her that according to their records, her giving wasn't what he/the church thought it should be. I don't know how the Pastor knew what this woman and her husband's giving should look like but after the shaming, the Pastor eventually gave her a gift card. I don't remember the amount, maybe $50?

At least her family had something to eat for that day. The reason the Pastor gave for eventually agreeing to help her was because she was a volunteer.

It makes sense to me to help your church staff and volunteers first, I get that. But to pull up her tithing records for a $50 Walmart gift card? Really? It makes me think… What was the point of shaming her? Was she not struggling enough?

Who decided what her tithing should be and how did they arrive at that amount? How many Pastors frequently look to see which members are tithers and which ones aren't? Are the non-tithers treated differently? My God!

In the present-day church setting where congregants are taught that their faith is the problem whenever they're in need, we can turn to the Bible and see where in the Book of Acts, the believers were taught the Word of God, but they were also fed and accommodated with whatever was needed.

The early Christian community established after Jesus' death and resurrection, found themselves pooling their money and resources together. It was then dispersed to the congregation based on what the individual needed, rather than on how much tithes they gave, or whether they had been through membership classes or not. The Bible, in Acts Chapter 2:44-45 describes the early church as having *'everything in common'*.

[4] And all who believed (who adhered to and trusted in and relied on Jesus Christ) were united and [together] they had everything in common;

[45] And they sold their possessions (both their landed property and their movable goods) and distributed the price among all, according as any had need.

The common thought around some evangelical camps is that anyone who doesn't have much or isn't living at a certain level financially, should do the necessary work of growing their faith and they're not afraid to let you know that. Faith does play a huge part in the life of a Believer in Christ because it is how we are commanded to live!

Galatians 3:11
New King James Version (NKJV)

[11] But that no one is [a]justified by the law in the sight of God is evident, for the just shall live by faith.

We live and walk by faith and not by sight!

2 Corinthians 5:7
New King James Version (NKJV)

[7] For we walk by faith, not by sight.

Even though we know these things to be true and we make our relationship with Jesus our number one priority, it is still possible to go to church full of hope and energy yet leave the service feeling condemned and almost lifeless based on the sermon you heard.

We mistakenly believed that a person's relationship with God was determined by their material possessions, and we thought that if someone was in need that was a sure sign that they didn't have a relationship with God.

If you showed up for a church service looking like something the cat dragged in, the common thought was that you needed one more scripture, and there was a huge possibility that you weren't a frequent tither or a volunteer.

Certainly, we all need to spend quality time in the Word of God in order to learn, grow, and develop a better relationship with Jesus Christ. However, if our first answer to someone's need is to point a finger at how much faith they do not have, and what they're doing wrong rather than trying to get them the help that is needed, then we need some help ourselves!

I am not saying that we're supposed to pay each other's bills every month; most people are trying their best and working hard, but at times they are unable to make ends meet, let alone prosper financially.

If someone is experiencing hard times that's the time to buy them some food if you're able to. The scriptures can come later, but for right now let's hold off on the mule of religion and attempt to help wherever we can.

WON'T HE DO IT?

Some people keep their needs between themselves and God alone, there's nothing wrong with that! Even though they didn't share their needs with someone on earth, that doesn't mean that God is unable to show out in their lives in a miraculous manner. He will do it as only He can!

As I'm writing right now, I am thinking of Pastor E. V. Hill who passed away many years ago. He once shared a testimony of one day when his mom didn't have any food for the family, yet she was trusting in God and had the dinner table prepared for a meal.

He kept asking his mom where the food was, and her reply was the same: *"God will supply what we need."* His mom had the table prepared and set for dinner even though there was nothing for her to cook!

Sure enough, Pastor Hill said it may have been an hour or two later, there was a noise on the balcony and someone that his mom had never seen before, showed up with several boxes of food! Yeah God! I can also remember in my own life back in the 90's when something similar happened to me.

The food I received was exactly what we needed! It was so detailed, down to my favorite box of tea and favorite brand of rice milk! God is so very faithful to us. Miracles do happen! God hears and answers our prayers. He even answers before we ask Him!

Isaiah 65:24
New King James Version (NKJV)

"It shall come to pass
That before they call, I will answer;
And while they are still speaking, I will hear."

God doesn't rain money out of the sky, He uses people to bless people; He uses people to help other people. There are people who aren't saved, don't care to know about Jesus, live their lives outside of the Bible, yet they fare much better than many Christians who are armed with scriptures and daily confessions.

Why is that? Well, they make good earthly decisions with their paychecks (and they don't even tithe). They do the practical things like budgeting, investing, saving, not living beyond their means, not overspending, etc.

FINANCIAL STEWARDSHIP

I've heard several sermons and various teachings about Financial Stewardship, but they have always been from the standpoint of giving to your church and being a good steward over your money in that way, by not neglecting the tithe, and the giving of offerings.

Depending on who's preaching the sermon and how deeply steeped they are in religion, you may even hear sermons about being a good steward by giving first fruit offerings, and maybe even a second fruit and a third! (It could get wild out there at times).

Very few churches teach their congregations about starting a business, writing and publishing their first book, forming a corporation or LLC., investing in the stock or foreign exchange markets, educating themselves about crypto currency, or even purchasing property. What we usually hear about financial stewardship comes from a one-sided view: continue to tithe and give offerings to this church and the Lord will bless you. Yes, it's true, God most certainly will!

However, the question remains, as a tithing member in good standing who is attending service every week or maybe twice per week: What avenues do you have ready and available to enable your wealth to flow to you? We know that our local churches have their storehouses; it's often preached to us before the tithes and offerings are collected:

Malachi 3:10
New King James Version (NKJV)

[10] Bring all the tithes into the storehouse,
That there may be food in My house,
And try Me now in this,"
Says the LORD of hosts,
"If I will not open for you the windows of heaven
And pour out for you such blessing
That there will not be room enough to receive it."

Do you have places to store your wealth? There is a transfer of wealth that has already begun and you're not going to miss out on it! I can almost guarantee that all our Pastors have wealth stored up somewhere; your Pastor is not broke! It's not all about giving to the church. That is not the only thing that our Pastors and ministry leaders did to become wealthy!

Many of them have online stores, brick and mortar stores, gold and silver investments, crypto currency that's being staked, money market accounts, stock and foreign exchange market accounts, oil wells, real estate etc. You and I can (and ought to) have those things as well! Does the average Christian have those things? Does the average Christian at least know how to go about getting those things? These are serious things for us to pay attention to. If we don't yet have wealth portfolios, do we even have any idea how to begin building them? Do we have more than a thousand dollars in a savings account? Crypto isn't everything, but would God be able to supernaturally transfer Bitcoin to our crypto wallets if we don't have one? We will need crypto wallets to enable those transactions.

Would God be able to show us what type of building to construct on the acreage we just purchased? We would need to have the acreage first. What about trading currency pairs or commodities? We need to be educated about all of it. If your answer to any of the above questions is no, then changes need to be made. Allow the Holy Spirit to lead you in these areas, and whatever He tells you to do, do it!

You and I both know that our churches will benefit when the wealth begins to flow into the accounts of the members, and more importantly, those in need will have food on their tables, their utilities will be paid up on time, their rent or mortgages and their vehicles will be paid up and paid off, and they'll be able to take exotic vacations just like everyone else! But until that happens, there will continue being church as usual, with the normal ten percent of the congregation carrying the other ninety percent, and acute shortages all around.

THE BLESSING OF THE LORD

The Blessing of the Lord makes us rich, and He adds no sorrow to the wealth He gives, but if we're judging our faith based on what we believe someone else has received from God, we're off to a horrible start. If you bought a new house and I'm renting an apartment, it's not smart for me to think that your faith is more than, or better than, or stronger than mine.

There are numerous situations, circumstances, and issues involved in someone receiving something *'from the Lord'*, that you and I know nothing of. The God-has-blessed-me lever gets pulled every time someone receives something, and we're often led to believe that this person prayed, fasted and was a faithful tither; therefore, this blessing from God was the result of all that they did. Except that's not always the case, and that's not how the Blessing of the Lord works. No one needs to pray or fast to obtain the Blessing. Scripture is clear that God sent Jesus to bless us.

Acts 3:26
New King James Version (NKJV)

[26] To you first, God, having raised up His Servant Jesus, sent Him to bless you, in turning away every one of you from your iniquities."

Maybe someone knew you had a need and they stepped in to help you. Maybe it's that your uncle bought you a vehicle, or your parents paid your rent. Or maybe it was your dad that gave you a starter house to live in, your sister paid your mortgage, and your auntie gave you a job. That's nice! If you and I have the unique privilege of being able to help a friend, family member or a stranger when they need it, then let's do it!

Spirit-filled believers with confessions, declarations, and perfect tithing records still go through divorces (the divorce numbers are alarming, especially in the Church.) Holy-Ghost filled people still have heart attacks, strokes and death occurring in their families. They still experience foreclosures, evictions and repossessions. The chances of financial hardship happening to your Pastor may be slim, but for the lay person those chances are higher. Why? It's simple.

Pastors often move in different circles and have more access to resources than most of their congregations do. Depending on the size of the church their salaries are most likely two to three times higher than yours too. As soon we come to the realization that everything that went wrong in our lives didn't go wrong because we left the choir, or because we didn't say our confessions every day, or because we didn't bless the Pastor, the easier things will become in our lives.

I've heard things like: *"Well, this happened to Bob because he wasn't a regular tither. That divorce happened to Karen because her faith wasn't strong enough. This sickness attacked Tonya because she didn't have a prayer life."* What went wrong when you kept tithing yet still experienced foreclosure, or why God blessed you with a car, but it ended up being repossessed may have nothing to do with your faith and everything to do with your decision making.

We live in a fallen world and sometimes we don't always make the right decisions about our money, or relationships, or our health. Trusting God doesn't mean that we will have answers to all of life's questions, but it does mean that we will come out of whatever situation we're in that seems impossible. It's time to be free of that narrow way of thinking, escape the harmful cycle of spiritual abuse and let your relationship with Jesus (not your relationship with your Pastor) be the energy that continually fuels your life.

It is possible to prosper *outside* of the will of God and nothing challenging will happen to you. You can also prosper *in* the will of God and experience pain and torment. The spirit of religion hovers in and around most churches on any given day, unchecked and unrestrained and this is because when you're not familiar with the Gospel of Grace, you'll always find religion to be a comfortable and familiar place to live. If religion is your comfort zone, the devil can come in with every type of scenario imaginable in order to convince us to believe his lies.

The comforts we experience in life are not always an indication of our obedience to God, or that we are living according to His will for our lives. The Word of Faith teaching that if you are in God's will everything will go well for you, that is a lie. That is not proof of being in God's will, as the Bible cites example after example of men and women who lost a lot, even the Apostle Paul who lost everything and didn't consider it because he knew he was living in the will of God.

SELLING JESUS

On any given night, we can witness televangelists on TV selling Jesus to the highest bidder. You may hear that if you give a certain amount of money to this person's ministry that this particular thing will happen to you within X number of days.

I fell for that foolishness once as a brand-new Christian and I tell the story in my E-Book, 'From Foolishness to Faith, One Woman's Journey'. I was at a church and the Guest Preacher said: *"If what you have in your hand is not enough to meet your need, then it's your seed.* Based on what the preacher said, my seed would be multiplied and quickly returned to me.

If I remember correctly, the harvest should come within 48 hours. The need I had at the time, was to pay the electric bill but I didn't have enough money to do so. What did I do? I gave the money that I had into the offering bucket believing that what the Preacher said would happen for me. I figured that he was the one hearing God and not me, I didn't know anything about hearing God yet, I was a brand-new believer in Christ.

I believed that the money I had in my hand, was my seed and that my faith would miraculously cause more than enough money to come back to me quickly. Instead, what did happen quickly was that the electric service was cut off. Guess who had to wait 2 days on another paycheck to pay the bill? You guessed it! If you're reading this and wondering what *'seed'* is, there is a common belief in evangelical circles that money (among other things) is seed, even though the Bible in Luke Chapter 8, verse 11 clearly tells us that: *"The seed is the Word of God."* That's why every born-again man or woman should develop a habit of continuously reading the Word of God (the seed) which would then cause the seed (the Word of God) to take root in the recreated spirit of the reader, which would then cause a harvest of the seed (Word of God) to manifest in many different areas of our lives. This doesn't happen overnight, but it does happen!

In Luke Chapter 8, verses 5-10 Jesus shares a parable about a sower who was sowing seed and described what happened to the seed as it was sown. Some of the seed fell on the wayside, some on rocks and some on thorns. But then He tells us that some of the seed fell on good ground, and He declared in verse 11, that the seed that He was talking about was really the Word of God.

Luke 8:11
King James Version (KJV)

11 Now the parable is this:
The seed is the word of God.

It is incumbent upon us, to read the Word of God for ourselves, and allow the Holy Spirit to show us exactly what the scriptures mean. At the same time, God has also given gifts to the Church, as listed in Ephesians Chapter 4 verses 7-13. The gifts of Apostle, Prophet, Evangelist, Pastor and Teacher have been given to the Church by God, and in a nutshell, their jobs are to nurture and prepare the Church to do its own ministry.

Your Pastor and mine have been given to us by God to teach us and help us to correctly interpret the

Word of God, so that we can walk it out in our daily lives and minister that Word to others, thereby building up the Church body.

The problem occurs when the spiritual leadership we're learning from don't have correct interpretation of the Word of God, and they preach and teach a gospel of religion to us, rather than the Gospel of Grace. Whole congregations are being led down ditches of religion, quoting, and declaring their favorite scriptures as they go down.

We can partly blame ourselves for some of these errors learned, because we're supposed to be reading the Word for ourselves and not just relying on our Pastors who are just as human as we are. I've found that the more we un-learn and unpack religion, the freer we become, and our prayer lives became so much better!

I started a blog back in 2013. It was a daily devotional, emailed to subscribers every day of the year for three years. Every time I would enquire of the Lord about whether it was time to change the main theme of the blog, I would be led to stay with what I was already doing, which was to remind us all to work on our relationship with Jesus.

I kept reminding my readers over and over to study the Word of God as often as possible, and let that Word grow in their hearts, because, as my Pastor says: *"Knowing the Word is knowing God."* This has always been the heart of God that we would grow to know Him better and better, so that it would become difficult for us to be deceived by the devil.

There are still churches who are pastored by men and women whose main concern is money and power, and what it can do for their image. Some Pastors are still deeply concerned about the number of people in their pews which for them translates into how much money hits the bank account on any given weekend because there are bills to pay.

I've experienced several gimmicks used during offering time, promising the givers things that God never promised: Sow $37.00 for Psalm 37 or give $150 for a praise offering because of Psalm 150, and if we did that, God would do something for us.

I've also heard that we would have the hundred-fold return on all our giving every time we gave an offering, and to activate that, we should give the largest offering we could give because we would receive it back multiplied by a hundred within thirty days. Those are gimmicks!

Those that came to church just to learn about Jesus, those who want to be taught the Word of God, those looking for real spiritual guidance become disappointed when things don't work out as they were told it would. We need the assistance of the Holy Spirit to help us to discern between right and wrong, and we need the mind of Christ in order to immediately recognize the traps so that we are no longer deceived.

Chapter 9

THE AFTERMATH

HIGHLIGHTING BLACK WOMEN:

KATHRYN JOHNSTON was a 92-year-old woman who was killed by police in a no-knock raid by Atlanta police. Officers broke down her security gate and without warning entered her home. She fired the pistol she kept for self-defense, hitting no-one. Officers fired back 39 times.

Officers later admitted to lying about finding cocaine at her house and planting marijuana at her house after the raid. The officers pleaded guilty to charges as well as the cover-up and received prison time. Rest in peace and power, Kathryn!

Anyone who's telling you they aren't seeing the state of the Church is either lying or may need to get their heads checked out. We must be able to come to terms with how we got here. What issues have been swept under the rug? What issues have we pretended that we haven't seen?

Sometimes in life, lines are crossed so flagrantly that the stand you took on the issue forever changes and defines you. For me, that line was watching the decisions made by the majority of church leaders concerning the 2016 and 2020 elections, as their decisions brought about the widening of the divide that we see today. The stand that most churches took, encouraging their congregants to vote is to be highly commended. Attempting to manipulate them to vote a certain way, isn't.

THE POLITICAL PARTY OF THE BODY OF CHRIST

It now seems that conservatism under President Trump (otherwise known as Trumpism) has been further narrowed by his rhetoric: The rhetoric of the Christian nationalist whose job is to protect the nation, the president and the Republican party with prayer and spiritual works.

When this group wins an election it's considered God's will, but when they lose it's considered the devil's work. Anyone that opposes that way of thinking gets left out of the group. Some are critics who aren't there to find proof in order to have their minds changed. They are there to fit whatever information is given out, into the narrative that they want to believe, which is that the Republican party is the party of the Body of Christ. (It saddens me to type this, but it must be said.)

Now we're here in the aftermath of the 2020 elections and I won't be surprised to soon hear sermons on unity and forgiveness (without repentance and/or apologies). There will be a general glossing over the nastiness of the last four years and the part that the Church played especially during the last two election cycles. Any acknowledgment of the harm that was caused by church leadership would be a dream come true for me, and if there was also an apology following it that would be icing on my cake.

If things continue as they have been for multiplied decades, and someone dares to speak out against the non- apologies we'll see the *'insubordination'* card pulled. That is the same insubordination card that gets pulled and thrown into your lap if you dare speak out against fear tactics and oppression in your local church or ministry.

The person attempting to speak out will most likely be told that they are *'causing strife'*. I must warn you because I have personally experienced it, that this, my friend, is the ultimate playbook of an abuser where the abuser blames you for being abused. Yep, it happens in churches and ministries too, beware!

In a church or ministry, if you are speaking out about fear tactics, oppressive leadership, racist leadership, or even the *'you-must-vote-Republican'* narrative, that is not what causes strife. One of the things that causes strife or conflict is when you're *not* allowed to speak up about wrongdoing. It's when your voice is not allowed to be heard, when you are prohibited from speaking up about matters that directly affect you.

That's when the tension begins to build up, frustration and angst settle in, and strife is the result. When the Church begins to restrict more than it provides freedom from mental torture that is when we have a problem and strife steps in.

James Chapter 3 verse 16 tells us what happens when strife shows up:

> **16 For where envying and strife is, there is confusion and every evil work.**

Strife is defined as: *Angry or bitter disagreement over fundamental issues; conflict.*

Are there more don'ts than dos at your local church? Are there frequent opportunities to shame others who don't conform to the church's ideology and practices? Are you left out of the clique if you don't dress like the First Lady does?

Does the peer pressure and social conditioning at your church make you squirm? Do you often leave church feeling more condemned than when you came in? That is what causes strife - bitter disagreements and anger over fundamental issues. That is what causes conflict.

FLIPPING TABLES - HOUSEWIVES FRANCHISE STYLE

As Christians we walk by faith and not by sight, and once we know we've heard from heaven, we hold on to what God says no matter what happens. Strangely enough, the 'walking by faith and not by sight' that the Church participated in before, during and now after the 2020 election cycle was nothing short of maniacal. Things started heating up about six months before the election, when the usual sermons were about which political party was acceptable to God, and why.

After the 2020 election I saw a video on Twitter where a Pastor told the congregation that what the Lord started talking to him about was: *"He went through, and He overturned the tables."* Unhappy with President Biden's win, the Pastor then simulated the Bible verse where Jesus flipped over tables in the temple.

There was a table on the church platform, and he then promptly flipped over the table (maybe to suggest that this is what would have happened if Jesus stood at the tables at the election office as the votes of the American people were being counted?) This action was in response to the deep desire of evangelicals to see the election results of November 2020 overturned. However, the actions of the Pastor completely misinterpreted the scripture (found in

Mark Chapter 11 verses 15-17) because Jesus turned over the tables of the money changers because they were in the wrong place selling their goods. He stopped them from using the Temple as their marketplace, as the Temple was supposed to be a *'House of Prayer for all nations'*. The election workers on the other hand, were just doing their job! It was their job to count (and re-count if necessary) the votes that came in.

This was a legitimate job! Jesus wouldn't be at the election office flipping over the tables of the election workers who were simply doing their jobs. They were counting votes cast by the American people! Why on earth would Jesus turn their tables over? But wait ... there's more! There were seventeen Republican Attorney Generals who stepped up to support the state of Texas as the Attorney General for Texas insisted on seeing the votes in predominantly Black areas overturned.

The Church was there leading the way in prayer: *"Lord, if need be, let there be another election!"* This is almost unbelievable! These Attorney Generals (and the praying conservative evangelicals) attempted to reverse the results of the 2020 elections because they didn't like the outcome! This is how cognitive dissonance plays out. The mind will do anything to hold on to the core belief (that was wrong in the first place.) The states of Pennsylvania, Michigan, Georgia and Wisconsin were sued simply because a large majority of Black people in the cities of Philadelphia, Detroit, Atlanta and Milwaukee voted against President Trump!

That the Church would get involved in what would be seen as casting doubt on the validity of votes coming out of predominantly Black communities could blow your mind if you let it. The Republican Attorney Generals doing their Republican thing, suing the states - that's one thing. Sure, go ahead!

But for the Body of Christ to be involved in further oppressing Black people by supporting the Attorney Generals in prayer to overturn the votes of Black people with their witchcraft prayers? Really? All of this in an attempt to make their prophetic words come to pass! We've hit that sunken place, people! (You'll have to either watch the movie *'Get Out' or* ask a woke Black friend to explain that movie). Either way, this behavior is un-Christ-like and totally unacceptable.

The bitter truth is that even though President Trump lost the election, the racism, bigotry, hatred, division and other evil forces that were resurrected by his tenure and with his words, will be with us for decades to come – unless the Church takes the lead in acknowledging their part, repenting, and moving forward as a changed Church with minds renewed by the Holy Spirit. If your spiritual leaders were a part of the group of evangelicals who preached about voting Republican because it best aligns with God's views, and those same leaders haven't said anything about the racism and bigotry they ended up supporting by their silence, it's time for you to ask yourself some serious questions about the love walk they've been preaching about.

PRAYER CHANGES THINGS AND PEOPLE, LET'S PRAY!

To the *'this is un-American'* crowd and the *'this is not who we are'* crowd, I have a message for you: America is not God's chosen nation above all nations (I know you may have heard that at your local church), and unfortunately it wasn't built with the idea of advancement for everyone either. The racist behavior we see today is consistent with the history of the United States. God didn't bring this nation into being in order to strip minorities of their families, rights, heritage, etc.

God didn't bring disenfranchisement and poverty to minorities while He allowed others to go free. This corrupt system of racism has benefited White Pastors and church leaders so it's much easier for them to say: *"Well let's pray about it,"* rather than doing something that would benefit their minority congregants.

I dearly love and believe in prayer, and I know that it changes things and people. We really should pray often. When I say that I'd rather pray than eat, I really do mean it. Prayer is my life, it's the main reason I'm here. However, the Church has been praying and expecting things to fall into place automatically: *"Lord heal racism in this nation, in Jesus' name we pray Amen."* We should be doing the work of doing.

What does that mean? It means doing the work of instituting change that matters. It means doing the work of seeking out justice. God is a God of justice. When will more White church leadership join us in our cry for change, justice or economic advancement?

VOTER FRAUD AND THE CHURCH

I believe that President Trump did a good thing by surrounding himself with a plethora of Christian right-wing Pastors, who I had hoped would have been able to share Godly wisdom with him, and maybe they did!

What I saw instead was that many were eager to lie to their congregations about what a great leader he was, chastised their congregations about speaking ill of the president because *"sometimes you say dumb things too."* Many church leaders shared the lies and misinformation with their congregations, and everyone was happy and in faith!

It wasn't long before President Trump's lies and misinformation became the Church's lies and misinformation except, it wasn't called that… the Church received the lies as truth!

So much so, that in 2016 when President Trump won the states of Michigan, Pennsylvania, and Wisconsin by 77,000 votes, the Church considered it to be a landslide victory, but in 2020 when Joe Biden won the same states: Michigan, Pennsylvania and Wisconsin by 255,000 votes, and won the popular vote by 6 million, suddenly the chant turned into *'voter fraud'*. You cannot make this stuff up!

Even before election-day many evangelicals had already believed that the elections would be fraudulent (because they'd been hearing that narrative from the White House all year long).

They still went on to vote anyway!

Many of this same crowd are those who also believed that the Covid-19 virus wasn't real, and that it was *"made up by the left."* Meanwhile many evangelicals were also among those who succumbed to the virus, many of them died.

But I digress, let's go back to the fraudulent elections and dig in:

- Election officials: 'No evidence of election fraud.'
- Cyber security officials: 'No evidence of election fraud.'
- Department of Homeland Security: 'No evidence of election fraud.'
- Legal experts: 'No evidence of election fraud.'
- Media: 'No evidence of election fraud.'
- United States Court system: 'No evidence of election fraud.'
- Evangelicals: *"We heard from God and the truth will come out before the inauguration. Stop the steal! This election is not valid! President Trump will remain president for four more years!"*

I do not believe that every evangelical feels this way or believes the lies, but it's disheartening because millions of them do! Many evangelicals are Jesus-loving, Bible-reading, faith-walking people who pray and listen to the Holy Spirit in their everyday lives, and aren't radicalized white supremacists, racists, or insurrectionists.

Neither are they anti-Trump, never-Trumper and all the other boxes of hate that there are out there. The problem comes in when spiritual leaders are the white supremacists and the racists. The problem comes in when spiritual leaders also believe the lies of voter fraud without any evidence and encourage their congregations to believe the lie as well.

This is serious! The Bible, in 2 Corinthians Chapter 5 verse 7 tells us that we should walk by faith and not by sight, so maybe these leaders don't need to see evidence of voter fraud. Maybe they just believe in a fraudulent election by faith? At this point who knows except for God?

Conservative evangelicals say that the liberal media twists what they say, and the liberal evangelicals say the same thing about the conservative media. The Church has been told for decades by their leaders that they should not listen to the media and many of them don't, so I'm guessing that they got their misinformation about election fraud from social media.

Wherever their information came from, it's shameful how much of the Church also embraced the fraudulent election claims and were holding out for another inauguration on March 4, 2021, which also did not come to pass. This was all taking place even after President Joe Biden and Kamala Harris were inaugurated on January 20th, 2021.

There were many prophetic words about the re-election of President Donald Trump in 2020 that have not come to pass (but could still happen according to those who, even in November 2021 were waiting on a second inauguration). The world has been watching and continues to watch as a large majority of the Church prostrates itself before President Trump and Trumpism.

The reputation of evangelicals is on the line, the reputation of word of faith preachers is also on the line, and the reputation of this nation is definitely on the line. The unbelieving world as well as many in the Church are watching the religious hypocrisy. The thought of the world not believing anything the Church has to say because of our hypocritical words and actions, makes me sad.

How did we get here? Church leaders led their congregations here, so church leaders should be the ones to step up to the plate and make it right again, but I don't believe that many of them will. Obadiah 3 mentions that *"the pride of your heart has deceived you,"* and I believe that pride will prevent many church leaders from saying to their congregations: *"I am sorry, I misled you, I made a mistake, please forgive me. Let's work together to make this right. How can I help you?"* If you're reading this book and your Pastor has said that (or something similar) to your congregation, then praise God, things are looking up!

"You cannot be a Christian and vote for President Trump!" "You cannot be a Christian and vote for Hillary

Clinton!" Evangelical leadership who previously worked together for many years suddenly found themselves in a Pro-Trump versus Anti-Trump war in the Church. Before President Trump entered the ring these two opposing sides sang the same hymns, read from the same Bibles and fellowshipped together! Then politics entered the ring and things got wild.

Even Stevie Wonder could see that the Democrats have been out for President Trump from Day 1. They went out of their way to hold his feet to the fire, maybe more so than with other presidents, and that could be because he began lying even before day zero of his tenure! Did President Trump make it easy for them to keep him accountable to the American voters? No. It turned out to be a nightmare for millions of people that lasted until January 20, 2021.

JANUARY 6, 2021 NEVER FORGET!

What was even sadder were the events of January 6, 2021 when large groups of Trump-supporting thugs and insurrectionists bulldozed their way into the Capitol. *"How could this have happened?"* said no-one ever!

If you paid attention in your prayer closet you would have known that something vicious was about to take place. If you were not paying attention in your prayer closet you still could have realized that something vicious was going to take place. If you are unsaved and not familiar with the voice of the Holy Spirit, you would have realized that something vicious was going to take place. Even if you were living under a rock, the vibrations being made by all of creation groaning, would have made you realize that something vicious was going to take place.

And it did. *"Be there. Will be wild!"* Those were the words of the then-president as he tweeted about the rally-turned-riot-turned-insurrection. The chaos of January 6, 2021 was carefully and methodically planned. There had been many advertisements of a Trump rally that would take place on January 6, 2021, the day where the Biden confirmation proceedings would take place.

Realizing that all their efforts thus far to overturn the elections proved to be invalid, the Church continued praying, believing God that His prophetic word (given by many leading prophets about President Trump remaining in office) would come to pass.

President Trump bless his heart, probably listened intently to the Pastors and spiritual leaders surrounding him with their words of prophecy, which guaranteed him another four years based on what they 'received from the Lord.' Based on their encouraging words, President Trump ramped up his plan through many nasty tweets and continued to engage his supporters in his plan to march to the Capitol on January 6th.. The prophetic word from the mouths of 'trusted Prophets' must come to pass, by any means necessary!

Some in the crowd had been whipped up into such a demonic frenzy, that I believe all they could see was Vice President Mike Pence hanging from their man-made gallows, and Speaker Nancy Pelosi killed. It seemed like that was part of the plan of the insurrectionists as they were egged on by President Trump, who was led by his spiritual leadership, rather than by the Holy Spirit.

Some of the speakers at the rally that day, (including President Trump) continued to further inflame and agitate the spirits of many of the Trump supporters. Vice President Mike Pence found himself in a dangerous position because President Trump's words about him (and his tweets before that day about Mike Pence) continued to provoke the already inflamed crowd.

Before the rally was over, the president called on his supporters to be strong and encouraged them to never concede defeat. He told them that he would walk to the Capitol with them, but instead he went back to the White House to take a seat and watch the insurrection unfold. Demonic manifestations of anger, outrage, irascibility and even confusion, were the order of the day as the march continued to the Capitol. Before long at the Capitol, the president was being rushed to a more secure place, as shouts of *"Hang Mike Pence,"* (for what they considered to be betrayal by him for not supporting the overturning of the election results) were echoing in the halls of the Capitol. The insurrectionists invaded the Capitol, overwhelming police and occupying offices.

Meanwhile members of Congress donned gas masks and were also whisked away to safety. This went on for hours, as three people died of medical emergencies. An officer was almost crushed to death as he tried to escape, and other police officers were beaten. The Police Union has reported that as many as 140 policemen were injured on that day.

Outside the Capitol, one White woman caught on tape was shocked at what was happening, exclaiming *"They are supposed to shoot BLM [Black Lives Matter] but now they are shooting patriots!"* Hmm. In her mind, she's correct, Black Lives Matter are the ones to be shot, not the insurrectionists. This woman is not alone in her thinking! According to FBI reports released after the insurrection, the Capitol police were not prepared for the rioters, looters, and insurrectionists. They were however, prepared to handle traffic. Dear God.

CAN WE ALL JUST GET ALONG?

Where does the Church stand in all of this? Well, outside of still waiting on a second inauguration, hopefully church leaders are poised to lead congregations towards the Word of God and away from the narrowness of conservatism. There cannot be peace without justice, so I am hopeful that the body of Christ can face the situation, address it, have needful discussions, and then move on.

Simply moving forward from the sordid actions of evangelical leaders during every election cycle would be putting yet another band-aid on the cancer of narrow conservatism that already exists.

We've already witnessed the wreckage of 2020, and 2021. It's time to get together and cross the divide. It's time for us all to try to get along, as Rodney King asked back on May 1, 1992. Can you reach out to your Trump-supporting family and make peace?

Can you reach out to your Biden-supporting co-worker and make peace? Or has the issue of pro Trump versus anti Trump drawn a line in the sand that could never be re-crossed? We will need to work together to bridge the gaps of inequity, inequality, racism, injustice and greed. We can do it!

Chapter 10

IN CONCLUSION

HIGHLIGHTING BLACK WOMEN:

ALBERTA SPRUILL was a 57-year-old woman who died after police conducted a "no-knock" raid at her home in error. Officers broke through her door and threw a concussion grenade while Alberta was getting ready for work.

She was handcuffed then later released when officers realized they were in the wrong place and that the information they were given (that guns and drugs were being stored in her apartment) was incorrect. She died of a heart attack 30 minutes later. Her death was ruled a homicide, but no official charges were filed. Rest in peace and power, Alberta!

If you board the wrong train and you realize it, running along the corridor of the train in the opposite direction is useless, because you're still on the same train and its direction hasn't changed. This is a picture of the Church right now. We're heading in the wrong direction whether we want to admit it or not. The good news is that we have the power to turn the train around in the right direction, but first, we need to recognize where we went off course, stop the train, and then turn it around.

Because so many people don't do it, whenever you do stand up for what you believe is right, you end up being marginalized. Especially women. It's been quite the journey for me, but I wouldn't trade it for anything because I don't want to ever be on the religious side of life. Life doesn't amount to anything much when you're in cahoots with the spirit of religion that induces narrowness. All you and I must do is take a stand! Jesus called us to a life of faith not a life of comfort, and taking a stand means that there will be major moments of discomfort, so we may as well get used to it.

I am not trying to ignite sedition in the local church, but I am attempting to wake us up to the spirit of the world that has invaded the Church, that is hell bent on attempting to ruin the body of Christ. Apathy, racism, injustice and religion that have been firmly embedded in our local churches for centuries, must be uprooted.

The body of Christ should not be known as Republican churches, and we do not need to tell congregations how to vote; teach us how to hear the

Holy Spirit, and we will know how to vote! I believe that much of that teaching stems from fear, and I don't believe we've yet seen the error of our ways in that regard.

Spiritual haughtiness is the *'our church can do it better'* spirit, that is first and foremost, a spirit of religion. The Hebrew meaning of the word religion is: a return to bondage. Most Word of Faith evangelicals believe that they are the ones performing better in every area, and that belief shoved us all into a box, separating us from other churches who didn't perform as well as we thought they should.

That separation, coupled with the Church's yearning to operate as the propaganda arm of the Republican political party, also helped to get us to where we are today. Look around and you'll see that in many churches, what used to be one, two or even three services every Sunday have been relegated to just one Sunday service, and that happened years before the Coronavirus ever showed up!

People didn't run from every church when they realized that their local church was operating as a Political Action Committee, but they did run from many churches. We blamed the devil, and we blamed the people, but we did not take a close look at ourselves, and what really caused people to leave our churches in droves.

SEED TIME AND HARVEST

Most people don't attend church to fight off intimidation, oppression and the political narrative of their Pastors. We attend church primarily to be taught the Word of God. My grandmother used to say that what goes around comes around. The Bible calls it seed time and harvest. We had the perfect illustration of seed time and harvest at the protests that erupted after the murder of George Floyd.

The harvest of riots reaped in Minnesota and every other similar harvest, came from the seeds of multiplied years of slavery, demonizing immigrants, discrimination, racism, attacking voting rights, as well as multiple other subtle micro-aggressions hovering over Black people in this nation for hundreds of years. The narrow conservative explanation for what happened in Minnesota after George Floyd's murder, is that the riots occurred because the devil doesn't want a revival in Minnesota.

It's the devil alright! It's the devil that has influenced church leaders to ignore centuries of racism in our churches, and it's the same devil that occupies pulpits all over the nation, still ruling and reigning in many churches with a Jim Crow anointing that steals, kills, and destroys minorities in our congregations.

I'm pretty sure the devil doesn't want revival anywhere, but what happened in Minnesota would have happened in any city in the United States where yet another Black man had been killed! This is harvest time for the United States from the seeds of racism and Jim Crow that were sown in the early days, and it's up to the church to take care of it, and not continue to push it under the rug again as has been done for centuries.

WHERE DO WE GO FROM HERE?
Conservatism

- Admit that we were wrong.
- Be willing to be uncomfortable in this quest for change.
- Don't make our political views into idols above the Lord Jesus Christ.
- Apologize.

Pastors, please apologize to your congregations. Repent before God. Your prophetic word was wrong. It's not the fault of your church members; it's your fault for allowing racism, Jim Crow, inequality, inequity and injustice to rein supreme in your church.

Begin again! This time we won't be starting over from scratch, we'll be starting over with wisdom, a lot of experience and help from the Holy Ghost. We will be *the* body of believers united because we're in love with Jesus, rather than in love with a political party, a platform, or a man.

It's okay to have our own opinions but unless we wake up from the carnal coma we were induced into and decide to work on our relationship with God first, we will be right back where we started.

Racism

Have the uncomfortable conversations with the racists in your family (you probably already know who they are).

Do the same thing in your church, even if the racist is your Pastor, church leader or Life/Cell Group Leader. Speak out more as you are led by the Holy Spirit. When you remain silent you are endorsing it. Don't allow anyone to shut you down for speaking out against racism.

Conduct soul searching missions. What are you willing to accept? Where do you stand on certain issues and why? Where do you draw the line?

Find out why you feel the way you do about certain people groups. Where did those thoughts and feelings come from? (Reminder: Racism is not an agree-to-disagree subject). Repent and change your own behavior. Repent before your church if you're a leader there.

Stop trying to figure out how to stop the protests and figure out how to stop police brutality. Educate yourself. Be kind. If you have Black friends and family, let them know that you support them. (I have a friend who told me one day, even before the George Floyd murder: *"I hope you know that I will never let anyone speak anything racist to you or about you. I'm with you."*). May we all have friends like her!

Keep your foot on the pedal, stay in the fight.

Call it out in a peaceful manner! Call out racism when you see/hear it, let people know their behavior is unacceptable to you. If the person doesn't understand that what they are saying and how they are thinking is racist, please help them to understand why it is! It's not divisive to call out white supremacy in the Church. What is divisive is when no-one, especially in leadership is working to eliminate it, and when no-one is addressing it in their congregations.

Racism is the elephant in the room that few Pastors want to touch, even though they're quick to talk about repentance, forgiveness and walking in the love of God. Black people have practiced forgiveness repeatedly for centuries; we have had to, in order to just live! Forgiveness is one thing and reconciliation is another. I would like to see reconciliation that involves repentance with changed behavior and changed narratives. If the church leadership is unable to do that then preaching about forgiveness is a waste of time.

Repentance must be practiced especially since the past five years have done so much to the Church's witness. Thank God nothing can taint the image of Jesus. He still is Lord of all Lords and King of all kings!

Holy Activism

Justice is Biblical, let's look at some scriptures that show us that God is a God of justice!

Job 34:12
Amplified Bible, Classic Edition (AMPC)

Truly God will not do wickedly, neither will the Almighty pervert Justice.

Psalm 33:5
Amplified Bible, Classic Edition (AMPC)

He loves righteousness and Justice.

Psalm 103:6
Amplified Bible, Classic Edition (AMPC)

The Lord executes righteous and Justice [not for me only, but] for all who are oppressed.

ADVOCATES OF CHANGE

Jesus was an influential activist with a voice that spoke into the lives of the city officials. There were occasions where His family and friends walked away from Him and talked trash about Him. Sometimes we need to take and maintain a stand for a just and right cause.

We can use our various platforms and social media profiles to be advocates and activists whether people agree with us or not. It's what we're supposed to do. How do we become social activists and advocates of change in a church that continues to cling to its political interests?

Well, consider that the people who sheltered Jews during the Holocaust were breaking the law. Harriet Tubman and the Underground Railroad broke the law. Rosa Parks broke the law. If saving friends, family and innocent people is breaking the law, should we break the law to protect people?

If standing up for truth and justice is breaking the law, should we break the law? If saving your children means that you are breaking the law, what would you do? Would you stand by and watch them die in the name of the law, or would you break the law? I am not inviting you to cause a ruckus, but if your church won't listen to your concerns about activism, conservatism, racism etc., then take it to the streets. I can guarantee that Jesus will meet you there.

If you are vocal in your support for civil and social justice, you aren't complaining, you're doing the right thing. I am asking you to consider what you would do in certain situations where you are required to take a stand. More people seem to be pointing fingers at activists and civil rights advocates without being in their shoes to understand their fight.

Activism isn't the easiest thing to do, but someone must take a stand! I'm thankful for protests, and solidarity marches and whatever else that must be done to state our case and stand for what we believe in. This is yet another reminder that non-protestors do not get a vote on how others should protest - leave it to them, you stay out of it because you are not the one that's protesting.

Staying away from activism isn't an option for many Black people because injustice is a part of our daily lives. If you have the option to ignore it, consider yourself among a privileged group because most Black and Brown people are unable to. Since Jesus was and still is on the side of the oppressed, He would advocate for freedom for the marginalized and disenfranchised. Many people in Republican-led churches don't see the marginalization. In their minds they're in the best local church ever, they love their leadership (as we all should) and everything is alright in their world. Someone in that crowd is always either 'overcoming', or 'waiting on manifestation', or 'praying out a prophetic word', or 'believing God', or 'blessed and highly favored'. I've done and said all those things, and all the while I was thinking to myself: *"You know what? I want some answers, real solid answers."* If you identify with my thoughts, I'd like for you to ask yourself the following questions and give yourselves honest answers:

-Is your life full of results? (From your tithing, prayers, giving, fasting, volunteering, or other spiritual works)?

-Are you having to constantly kiss up to your spiritual leaders in order to be promoted, or to sing on the praise team, or to lead a prayer group?

-Do you believe that eventually a leader will see how hard you've been working and give you the promotion at your church that you've been longing for?

-Can you (if you're not in a leadership position) make an appointment to see a Pastor on staff or maybe even the senior Pastor, and actually see him/her?

-When someone decides to leave the local church or ministry, does the Pastor/any leader speak against the person because they left the church or Ministry? (If that's happening in your church, I need you to know that that is a fear tactic to also keep you from leaving).

-Are the words of prophecy you're constantly hearing really coming to pass as declared? Or are you blamed when they don't come to pass? Do you hear things like: You didn't pray hard enough, you didn't pray long enough, you didn't sow a seed with your prayer, or you didn't 'wage a good warfare?'

-Do you frequently hear prayers that bless one political party but demonize the other?

-Do you hear words of prophecy that are laced with religion? Do they sound like, *'If you do this, God will do that, but if you don't do this, God won't do that?'*

If you answered yes to any of the above questions, pray this with me:

Heavenly Father, I want results.
I've been praying and confessing things for years, but I don't have half of the results that I know you want me to have.

Please show me where I went wrong and help me to get on the right pathway.

I want my relationship with you to be as authentic and as meaningful as possible without religious deception, cliques and political grandstanding.

Teach me how to pray and how to be led by Your Spirit, in Jesus' name I pray, amen!

LET'S DISRUPT THE SYSTEM!

I am a full-time disruptor here to disrupt belief systems, thought patterns and the status quo among other things. There will be times in our lives where we'll have to make up our minds about attempting to turn some ungodly systems upside down. I used the word 'attempt,' because it won't happen with just one person, but you'll be able to make a dent for sure! Systems of injustice and the hierarchy of racism and religion in our local churches must come down.

As Christians, we must be disruptors of narrow conservatism as well; else we will continue to go around in circles for another couple of decades. We'll have to challenge the status quo and become spiritual revolutionaries who walk this out.

You may have heard that we should only protest in our prayer closets but to me that's laughable. Prayer is absolutely necessary, but faith-filled prayers without works is what we've done for decades, and it keeps the church in status-quo mode, going around the same mountains. That must stop! What if Martin Luther King Jr. protested only in his prayer closet? What if Rosa Parks did the same thing? And Representative John Lewis? And Harriet Tubman? Where would the nation be right now? For sure, Black and African American people would still be drinking out of different water fountains from that of White people.

We must ask ourselves and others the hard questions, then demand answers and ask more hard questions until we get to the bottom of this. Keep pushing until something or someone moves in the right direction. None of us should remain silent just because our voices would make someone feel uncomfortable.

FINALLY

The sole purpose of this book is to reveal how narrow and restrictive our lives become when we manipulate and coerce each other into choosing political sides and identifying ourselves by those and other labels. I know that this may be an affront to you if you consider yourself to be conservative, but I hope that as you read through these pages, you realized that *'conservative'* is just another label that we've placed upon ourselves in the Church and that because of labels, the Church has been split into so many different directions that it has become challenging to recognize us anymore as one body, the Body of Christ. I'm convinced that because we have chosen to affiliate ourselves with labels that identify us in a certain way, that the demonic mannerisms and character traits that are attached to those labels, have now become the major identifying factors of the Church! It doesn't have to be that way though.

We are Christians, born again into a new life in Christ. Period. At the very least I hope that you would consider that there is so much more to your spiritual life than constricting yourself to this or any other narrow and oppressive way of thinking and being. You are a Christian that's what this book is all about.

WHAT'S YOUR STORY?

I am in favor of everyone writing their own story. There can never be too many books in my opinion. The history we read today was told by someone who put their personal slant to it, whatever that may have been. Who but God knows if one hundred years from now reading a history book about Covid-19 could leave the reader believing that it was just a sneeze that took the lives of just a few people?

Depending on who writes the history of today, the season that the Church is in right now could be sanitized and romanticized, as was done with Dr Martin Luther King, Jr. and his history.

Depending on who writes the story, in fifty years we could read articles about the January 6 2021, insurrection and it may sound as though a few people conducted a peaceful rally on the Capitol steps. Or George Floyd's murder could be told as thought it was just another Black man selling drugs who shot at law enforcement, and they killed him in return.

Please write. Write more, write often, write your history and tell your story. Tell the world how you see it and generations to come after you will be able to read your story, see history through your eyes, and taste your legacy and experience it from the depths of your soul!

This book wasn't written to bash a political party, neither was it written to bash the Church. I am a vital part of the body of Christ and if you are a born-again Christian, then you are a vital part too! I see this book as a wake-up call for the Church similar to the way in which I was awakened 3 times on the morning of March 6, 2017 with the words, *'The Narrowness of Conservatism'*, and eventually realized that it was an assignment for me at this season of my life. I have now completed this part of that assignment, but I am aware that the journey has only just begun.

TRADITION MAKES THE WORD OF GOD OF NO EFFECT

I want the body of Christ to take an inward look and see that we don't need all the labels we've been clinging to, labels that divide the body of Christ.

I understand that our labels are traditions that go back several generations and most of us would hate to give them up, but I am also aware that Jesus said that our traditions hinder the Word of God and cause His Word to have zero effects in our lives.

Mark 7:13
New King James Version (NKJV)

Making the Word of God of no effect through your tradition which you have handed down. And many such things you do.

If you desire unity and I'm hoping that you do, then let's get to work. Let's not confuse unity with uniformity. This isn't a *'separate but equal'*, experience for the Church. This is us, the body of Christ; we are one in Christ with individual cultures and experiences.

We never have to hide, shift or change our individual experiences because someone else doesn't understand it. It's okay if they don't understand you, and it won't be an issue as long as they're committed to loving you unconditionally anyway. Somewhere along the line our believing is what separated us when really, our believing is the force that was supposed to unite us! Believing in Jesus Christ, believing in His Word, believing in the power of His cross, that is where we started off as Christians.

If we focus on loving unconditionally as Jesus did and allowing the Holy Spirit to deal with people, their habits, their lives, and their vote, we could be off to an awesome start! God's Spirit didn't give us the job of policing each other; He asked us to believe in Jesus and unconditionally love each other.

The world is hungry for a Christianity that thinks well of God. Let's show them Who He really is, by how we treat them and each other. When I stand before God, I don't want my only response to be, *"But my Pastor said."* I want to be so familiar with my Savior here on earth, that when I see Him face to face, I can safely melt into His arms.

There won't be a strange or foreign feeling when I am in His presence. There won't be a feeling that I'm meeting someone that I'm vaguely familiar with. For this is the greatest love affair of all times manifesting in earthly and heavenly places at the same time.

My Savior, and me!

For more information about Sherma Jacqueline Felix, this book, or about the upcoming Workbook 'Conservatism Blackout,' please contact us at:

www.shermajacqueline.com

Made in United States
North Haven, CT
04 March 2022

16774849R00147